# Innovation in the Arts

IØ474425

This concise guide aims to increase what we understand by innovation in the arts and identify and support opportunities and strategies for the unique ways in which artists and arts administrators think about, engage in, and pursue successful innovation in their diverse creative practice.

Innovations in the Arts are often marginalised from a research perspective, in part because of the lack of a sound and compelling theoretical framework to support and explain process distinctions from business and management innovation. This book identifies three key concepts – art innovation, art movement innovation, and audience experience innovation – supported by formal theory for each concept presented and evidenced through case studies in art history. In this way, the book enables readers to identify, explain, and support their innovation efforts as visual, literary, and performing artists and arts administrators. It also explores strategies for pursuing innovation in practice.

Drawing attention to the unique ways in which artists and arts administrators think about and engage in innovation, this readable book will be an essential reading for students in all aspects of the creative and cultural industries and an essential guide to developing and promoting innovation in the arts for practitioners and researchers alike.

**Dr. Jason C. White** is an Assistant Professor and the Director of the Arts Administration program in the Department of Art at Xavier University, USA, where he prepares students for diverse careers in arts management and administration.

**Routledge Focus on the Global Creative Economy**
Series Editor: Aleksandar Brkić
*Goldsmiths, University of London, UK*

This innovative short-form book series aims to provoke and inspire new ways of thinking, new interpretations, emerging research, and insights from different fields. In rethinking the relationship between creative economies and societies beyond the traditional frameworks, the series is intentionally inclusive. Featuring diverse voices from around the world, books in the series bridge scholarship and practice across arts and cultural management, the creative industries, and the global creative economy.

**Innovation in the Arts**
Concepts, Theories, and Practices
*Jason C. White*

"Dr. White is a brilliant theorist with a tenacious desire to make theory applicable and effective when put into action. Readers will find this to be supremely true in his book Innovation in the Arts: Concepts, Theories and Practices. For those looking for guidance on how to understand and implement innovation in the context of the arts, this book is an indispensable guide and an essential resource."

**Jonathan Gangi,** *The Pennsylvania State University, USA*

"Dr. Jason C. White's Innovation in the Arts: Theories, Concepts, and Practices is a welcomed and significant contribution. Not only does the book build linguistic consensus previously lacking in the arts entrepreneurship literature around key terms, but it theorizes key processes necessary for the discipline's future advancement and success."

**Antonio C. Cuyler,** *Florida State University, USA*

"This is a very much-needed book for arts entrepreneurship scholars and those interested in becoming arts entrepreneurs. This book lays the groundwork for advancing arts entrepreneurship theories by clarifying the most fundamental concepts and early theoretical endeavors in this field. Moreover, this book offers critical resources and perspectives to inspire conversations on research and practices that advocate for artists and arts entrepreneurs of color."

**Wen Guo,** *Elon University, USA*

"Art is always changing and consistently never the same. Dr. Jason C. White reminds us of something important: that in addition to innovation prescribed in standardized conventions from the top, downward in business management, White shows that innovation also springs fresh from the unique practices of artists and arts administrators."

**Clayton Funk,** *Ohio State University, USA*

# Innovation in the Arts

Concepts, Theories, and Practices

Jason C. White

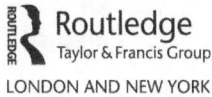

Routledge
Taylor & Francis Group

LONDON AND NEW YORK

First published 2023
by Routledge
4 Park Square, Milton Park, Abingdon, Oxon OX14 4RN

and by Routledge
605 Third Avenue, New York, NY 10158

*Routledge is an imprint of the Taylor & Francis Group, an informa business*

*British Library Cataloguing-in-Publication Data*
A catalogue record for this book is available from the British Library

*Library of Congress Cataloging-in-Publication Data*
Names: White, Jason C., 1982- author.
Title: Innovation in the arts : concepts, theories, and practices / Jason C. White.
Description: Abingdon, Oxon : Routledge, [2023] | Includes bibliographical references and index.
Identifiers: LCCN 2022017226 (print) | LCCN 2022017227 (ebook) | ISBN 9780367688776 (hardback) | ISBN 9780367695859 (paperback) | ISBN 9781003142393 (ebook)
Subjects: LCSH: Creation (Literary, artistic, etc.) | Artists--Psychology. | Arts administrators--Psychology. | Creative thinking. | Organizational change.
Classification: LCC NX160 .W49 2023 (print) | LCC NX160 (ebook) | DDC 700.1/9--dc23/eng/20220621
LC record available at https://lccn.loc.gov/2022017226
LC ebook record available at https://lccn.loc.gov/2022017227

ISBN: 978-0-367-68877-6 (hbk)
ISBN: 978-0-367-69585-9 (pbk)
ISBN: 978-1-003-14239-3 (ebk)

DOI: 10.4324/9781003142393

Typeset in Times New Roman
by MPS Limited, Dehradun

# Contents

# About the Author

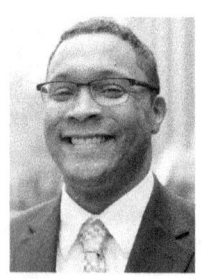

**Dr. Jason C. White** is currently an Assistant Professor and the Director of the Arts Administration program in the Department of Art at Xavier University, where he prepares students for diverse careers in arts management and administration. An accomplished researcher, educator and theorist, White is a published author in *Artivate: A Journal of Entrepreneurship in the Arts*, *Journal of Arts Entrepreneurship Education*, *Journal of Arts Management, Law and Society*, *Innovative Higher Education*, and *Arts Education Policy Review*. White is one of the co-creators of the Undergraduate Standards for Arts Administration Education (AAAE), and a founding member of the Society for Arts Entrepreneurship Education (SAEE). Artistically, White is best known as the playwright, co-actor, and co-director of the multi-award nominated and NAACP award-winning educational play, *The Dance: The History of American Minstrelsy*. Prior to receiving his PhD in Arts Administration, Education, and Policy from the Ohio State University, White earned a BFA in Acting from the California Institute of the Arts and attended the University of Akron; obtaining both a Masters degree in Arts Administration and a Masters degree in Educational Assessment and Evaluation.

# Acknowledgments

This book would not have been completed without the assistance of Dr. Jonathan Gangi, Dr. Wen Guo, Dr. Antonio Cuyler, Dr. Clayton Funk, and Dr. Gretchen McIntosh. Thank you all for volunteering your time to listen to my thoughts, read my late-night text messages, and offer constructive criticism to earlier drafts of this book. I'd also like to acknowledge my Lord and Savior Jesus Christ, because I prayed to him for the wisdom of Solomon, and he allowed me to receive it. There is absolutely no way I could have made sense of these particular innovation concepts, theories, and practices without his help. Lastly, I would like to thank my loving and supportive wife Dr. Ashley A. Roberts for somehow always finding the time to listen to my ideas and support my special projects. You are all greatly appreciated!

# 1   Introduction

## The purpose of this book

The purpose of this book is to increase your understanding of how innovation in the arts takes place by introducing and discussing three associated concepts. A formal theory for each concept is presented and evidenced through case studies in art history. These formal theories will help you to identify, explain, and support innovation efforts undertaken by visual, literary, and performing artists (collectively hereafter referred to as *artists*) and arts administrators. In addition, these theories will help you to shed light on and demystify common strategies for pursuing innovation in the arts within diverse art worlds and related industries.

## The need for this book

As a professor of arts administration, I've often noticed that when artists and arts administrators talk about innovation, they tend to describe and explain the concept in ways that differ from those provided by published scholars in the business management literature. This book was written to draw attention to the unique ways in which artists and arts administrators think about and engage in innovation practice. It was also written to fill a gap in the mainstream innovation literature, which tends to omit direct observations of innovation efforts undertaken by those who identify as artists and arts administrators.

After all, throughout art history, there are numerous examples of artists who developed and introduced new art forms, which is a form of process innovation. There are numerous examples of artists who organised and led art movements, which is a form of social innovation. There are numerous examples of arts administrators who developed

DOI: 10.4324/9781003142393-1

new kinds of experiences for arts audiences, which is a form of experience innovation.

Unfortunately, such efforts are rarely referenced as case studies in the mainstream innovation literature. In addition, concepts of *innovation in the arts* tend to be marginalised in peer-reviewed innovation journals, in part because these concepts are often included without reference to a compelling and sensible theoretical framework to support or evidence their existence. Further, without formal theories which help to explain process distinctions between business innovation and innovation in the arts, innovation efforts in the arts will continue to be marginalised in the broader innovation literature.

## Components of a theory

Although there are many published definitions, Frank Kerlinger (1986) defines a theory broadly as "a set of interrelated concepts, definitions and propositions that present a systematic view of phenomena by specifying relations among variables."[1] Laura Varpio et al. suggest that there are many different types of theories.[2] For example, descriptive theories describe the characteristics of phenomena. Explanatory theories clarify relationships between phenomena. Emancipatory theories articulate the oppression of a group of people. Disruptive theories extend existing knowledge or refute it. Predictive theories predict an outcome based on new findings. Theories can be broad in scope (e.g., grand theory), middle-ranged, or individually attributed. In the book *Reason and Rigor*, authors Sharon Ravitch and Matthew Riggan present a scenario helpful for increasing our understanding of what a theory is:

> Picture yourself in a room, looking at a page upon which you have drawn two boxes, the first labeled X, the second Y. There is a line connecting the two boxes. That line represents a relationship of some sort. What you are looking at is a theory.[3]

As Ravitch and Riggan suggest, theories provide us with an explanation for the relationship between two or more variables. We can choose to use this explanation to support our assumptions and beliefs about specific phenomena of interest. For example, Albert Einstein's theory of relativity can explain how space (i.e., variable 1) and time (i.e., variable 2) are linked (i.e., the relationship) for objects that are moving at a consistent speed in a straight line. A theory can explain why the sky is blue; plausibly gasses and particles in the earth's atmosphere scatter sunlight in all directions, and blue light is scattered more than other colors because it travels as shorter, smaller waves. A theory can help us to understand why adults who grow up in high-income areas have higher rates of arts participation than adults who grow up in low-income areas; plausibly access to K-12 arts education is a positive factor of influence on arts participation, and children who grow up in high-income areas have greater access to K-12 arts education than children who grow up in low-income areas. As you can see, theories can stimulate and guide the development of new knowledge. Theories can aid us in understanding things that we presently do not understand. Theories can help us to consider plausible answers to complex questions. Theories can provide us with a sensible and compelling rationale for the way something works.

Theories can also help us to understand different viewpoints of a social problem or issue. For example, according to new understandings derived from Richard Delgado and Jean Stefancic, critical race theory helps us to consider the impact of systemic racism from the perspectives of those who experience its negative effects.[4] Although there are various reasons, in general theorists tend to develop theories in order to offer a better description or explanation of something. Ravitch and Riggan provide support for this position when they state, "Nearly everyone agrees that theory attempts to explain why things work the way they do, and that it usually does so by way of identifying and examining relationships among things."[5]

## How are theories developed?

Theories are developed every day. When we wake up in the morning, we often theorise informally how our day is going to go based on how it usually goes or based on what we know or think we have to accomplish that day. Such theories like this are useful because they guide and inform our everyday decisions, actions, and behaviors. In the book *Designing Qualitative Research*, authors Catherine Marshall and Gretchen Roseman refer to these types of theories as *tacit theories* because they refer to personally held ideas about how things work or will work.[6]

Marshall and Roseman refer to theories found in the research literature as *formal theories* or *theories that are expressed in a formal manner and that are testable through at least one research study*. Formal theories are made up of concepts, or *one or more abstract ideas or general notions*. They include assumptions or *things accepted as true without much proof*. They include generalisations or *statements derived from the inference of specific cases*. They also include definitions, or *statements of the meaning of a word, word group, sign, or symbol*.

In general, formal theories are often developed by first (a) identifying a phenomenon of interest. Then, (b) identifying what is known and unknown about that phenomenon. Then by (c) identifying and analyzing relevant case studies. Through these activities, new knowledge about the phenomenon of interest is acquired, which helps prepare theorists for theory development.

Next, theorists will usually select a methodology useful for guiding their theory development process. There are a lot of methodologies to choose from, and each has its own strengths and weaknesses. One example is the hypothetico-deductive method, or hypothesis testing using the traditional scientific method. Another method is inductive reasoning or using specific observations to develop general conclusions or theories. Another is deductive reasoning or using generalisable conclusions to test hypotheses on specific cases. Another is the grounded theory method, or developing theory through iterative rounds of qualitative data collection and comparative analysis.

After developing a formal theory, theorists may choose to present that theory for public consideration and/or peer critique. In most of the research literature, the presentation of a new formal theory tends to include a **_theoretical framework_**; *a written argument or narrative that identifies the need, underlying logic, and rationale for the proposed theory.* In addition to stimulating discourse about a theory, theoretical frameworks can help readers to connect theorists' assertions and propositions to supporting citations in the research literature.

While theory is often perceived by the general public as an educated guess that seems logical, researchers often evaluate the quality of a formal theory (e.g., good, bad, weak, strong) by way of an assessment of the strengths and weaknesses of its supporting theoretical framework. Researchers may consider a formal theory to be of low quality if the supporting theoretical framework fails to justify the need for theory development, lacks relevant supporting citations, and/or does not offer an explanation that most members in a field consider to be logical. Alternatively, researchers may consider a formal theory to be of high quality if the supporting theoretical framework identifies the need for theory development, provides relevant supporting citations that strengthen a theorist's argument, and/or offers an explanation that most members in a field consider to be logical.

## Toward formal theory development

There are many theories published in both the innovation and related entrepreneurship literature that may help inform our understanding of innovation in the arts. For example, in theory, entrepreneurs like to be the first to exploit new economic opportunities because as *First Mover Theory* suggests, "new entrants who are early entry to a market niche will get advantages that include brand awareness and a reputation for being innovative."[7] Similarly, artists like to exploit opportunities to create art, and artists who create new art forms tend to be branded as pioneers in the arts and tend to gain a reputation for being innovative in art worlds.[8] Saras Sarasvathy's theory of effectuation offers us an explanation of how some innovators and entrepreneurs think, as well as a new way to analyze the behavior of innovators and entrepreneurs.[9] Research by Jonathan Gangi and Linda Essig suggests that artists tend to think just like innovators and entrepreneurs by using effectual thinking when creating art.[10] Everett Rodgers' theory of the diffusion of innovations offers us a comprehensive explanation of how product and process innovations get widely adopted by individuals and organisations overtime.[11] Research by Fariborz Damanpour and Marguerite Schneider suggests that organisational leaders frame innovation as organisational change.[12] They infer that the characteristics of managers and administrators of arts organisations (hereafter referred to as arts administrators) can influence arts organisations' rate of adoption.[13] Based on the endorsement of these theories by many innovation scholars, theory development seems to be necessary for advancing our knowledge and understanding of diverse innovation processes and practices.[14,15] As there are few published formal theories that explain how innovation takes place in art worlds, this book fills a gap in the broader innovation literature and the emerging arts innovation literature.[16]

## The need for mutual understanding

Before moving forward, it's important to make sure that I'm using language and terms that are mutually understood. This mutual understanding is necessary because despite over one hundred years of published innovation scholarship, most scholars still lack consensus on what innovation is.[17,18] This is because the concept of innovation can be framed in a wide variety of ways (e.g., process innovation, product innovation, experience innovation, organisational innovation). The concept of the arts can also be framed in a wide variety of ways. Depending upon who you are talking to, a reference to *"the arts"* may be a reference to one or more specific art forms, only those art forms recognised by social elites , specific arts-based fields, specific arts-based industries, one or more arts or cultural sectors, a subset of proposed creative or cultural industries, one part of a cultural economy, or one or more art worlds.

To add to the confusion, most people tend to think about the arts from their own cultural perspectives, rather than from the cultural perspectives of others. For example, when considering the arts, art historians in both Europe and the United States have historically tended to omit certain forms of popular entertainment. When considering the arts, art historians in India have historically tended to include etiquette, culinary arts, the art of weaponry and war, knowing how to compose and scan verses, arithmetic, knowing how to guess the human character from conduct and gestures, cosmetics, bed-making, wine preparation, and the making of artificial flowers.[19] Given that the arts refers to a specific context of innovation in this book, and given that the concept of the arts is often shaped and influenced by one's own cultural perspective, a mutual understanding is necessary.

To facilitate, I'll begin by specifying how the arts will be defined in this book, and then identify key terms utilised throughout this book. For easier identification, key terms will be bolded the first time they are presented, and the selected definitions that follow will be italicised. For those already familiar with these key terms, please skip to the concepts of interest discussed at the end of chapter 2.

Also, please note that this book includes an unusually high number of citations for a book that claims to be an accessible introduction for students and practitioners alike. While the high number of citations may seem intrusive to some readers, I feel the citations are necessary because they will point you to research findings that support my assumptions and provide proper credit to the authors of the words and ideas I use to communicate my conclusions. It is also important to publicly recognise the shoulders of the researchers, educators, theorists, and practitioners I am standing on, of which without, this book would not exist.

## Notes

1 Fred Kerlinger N., *Foundations of Behavioral Research*, 3rd ed. (New York, NY: Holt, Rinehart & Winston, 1986), 9.
2 Laura Varpio et al., "The Distinctions Between Theory, Theoretical Framework, and Conceptual Framework," *Academic Medicine* 95, no. 7 (2020): 989–94, 10.1097/ACM.0000000000003075.
3 Sharon Ravitch M. and Matthew Riggan, *Reason & Rigor: How Conceptual Frameworks Guide Research* (Thousand Oaks, CA: Sage Publications, 2012), 17.
4 Richard Delgado and Jean Stefancic, *Critical Race Theory*, 2nd ed. (New York, NY: New York University Press, 2012).
5 Ravitch and Riggan, *Reason & Rigor: How Conceptual Frameworks Guide Research*, 16.

6 Catherine Marshall and Gretchen B. Rossman, *Designing Qualitative Research* (Thousand Oaks, CA: Sage Publications, 2006).
7 Andre Laplume and Sepideh Yeganegi, *Entrepreneurship Theories*, Kindle (entrepreneurshiptheories.com, 2019), 59.
8 Victoria D. Alexander, *Sociology of the Arts: Exploring Fine and Popular Forms* (Malden, MA: Blackwell, 2003), chap. 8.
9 Saras D. Sarasvathy, *Effectuation: Elements of Entrepreneurial Expertise* (Cheltenham, UK: Edward Elgar, 2008).
10 Johnathan Gangi, "The Synergies of Artistic and Entrepreneurial Action," *The Journal of Arts Management, Law, and Society* 45, no. 4 (2015): 247–54, 10.1080/10632921.2015.1088912; Linda Essig, "Frameworks for Educating the Artist of the Future: Teaching Habits of Mind For Arts Entrepreneurship," *Artivate: A Journal of Entrepreneurship in the Arts* 1, no. 2 (2013): 65–77; Linda Essig, "Means and Ends: A Theory Framework for Understanding Entrepreneurship in the US Arts and Culture Sector," *The Journal of Arts Management, Law, and Society* 45, no. 4 (2015): 227–46, 10.1080/10632921.2015.1103673.
11 Everett M. Rodgers, *Diffusion of Innovations*, 5th, Kindle ed. (New York, NY: Free Press, 2003).
12 Fariborz Damanpour and Marguerite Schneider, "Characteristics of Innovation and Innovation Adoption in Public Organizations: Assessing the Role of Manager," *Journal of Public Administration Research and Theory* 19, no. 3 (2009): 495–522, 10.1093/jopart/mun021.
13 Fariborz Damanpour and Marguerite Schneider, "Characteristics of Innovation and Innovation Adoption in Public Organizations: Assessing the Role of Manager," *Journal of Public Administration Research and Theory* 19, no. 3 (2009): 495–522, 10.1093/jopart/mun021.
14 Sarasvathy, *Effectuation: Elements of Entrepreneurial Expertise.*
15 Everett M. Rodgers, *Diffusion of Innovations.*
16 George Swede, "Poetic Innovation," in *The International Handbook on Innovation* (Oxford, UK: Elsevier Science Ltd, 2003), 471–84.
17 Larisa V. Shavinina, "Understanding Innovation: Introduction to Some Important Issues," in *The International Handbook on Innovation* (Kidlington, Oxford: Elsevier Science Ltd, 2003), 3–16.
18 Fang Zhao, "Exploring the Synergy between Entrepreneurship and Innovation," *International Journal of Entrepreneurial Behavior & Research* 11, no. 1 (2005): 25–41, 10.1108/13552550510580825.
19 Arindam Chakrabarti, ed., *The Bloomsbury Research Handbook of Indian Aesthetics and the Philosophy of Art* (Bloomsbury Academic, 2018).

## References

Alexander, Victoria D. *Sociology of the Arts: Exploring Fine and Popular Forms*. Malden, MA: Blackwell, 2003.
Chakrabarti, Arindam, ed. *The Bloomsbury Research Handbook of Indian Aesthetics and the Philosophy of Art*. London, UK: Bloomsbury Academic, 2018.
Damanpour, Fariborz, and Schneider, Marguerite. "Characteristics of Innovation and Innovation Adoption in Public Organizations: Assessing the

Role of Manager." *Journal of Public Administration Research and Theory* 19, no. 3 (2009): 495–522. 10.1093/jopart/mun021

Delgado, Richard, and Jean Stefancic. *Critical Race Theory*. 2nd ed. New York, NY: New York University Press, 2012.

Essig, Linda. "Frameworks for Educating the Artist of the Future: Teaching Habits of Mind For Arts Entrepreneurship." *Artivate: A Journal of Entrepreneurship in the Arts* 1, no. 2 (2013): 65–77.

Essig, Linda. "Means and Ends: A Theory Framework for Understanding Entrepreneurship in the US Arts and Culture Sector." *The Journal of Arts Management, Law, and Society* 45, no. 4 (2015): 227–46. 10.1080/10632921.2015.1103673

Gangi, Johnathan. "The Synergies of Artistic and Entrepreneurial Action." *The Journal of Arts Management, Law, and Society* 45, no. 4 (2015): 247–54. 10.1080/10632921.2015.1088912

Kerlinger, Fred N. *Foundations of Behavioral Research*. 3rd ed. New York, NY: Holt, Rinehart & Winston, 1986.

Laplume, Andre, and Yeganegi, Sepideh. *Entrepreneurship Theories*. Kindle. entrepreneurshiptheories.com, 2019.

Marshall, Catherine, and Rossman, Gretchen B. *Designing Qualitative Research*. Thousand Oaks, CA: Sage Publications, 2006.

Ravitch, Sharon M., and Matthew Riggan. *Reason & Rigor: How Conceptual Frameworks Guide Research*. Thousand Oaks, CA: Sage Publications, 2012.

Rodgers, Everett M. *Diffusion of Innovations*. 5th, Kindle ed. New York, NY: Free Press, 2003.

Sarasvathy, Saras D. *Effectuation: Elements of Entrepreneurial Expertise*. Cheltenham, UK: Edward Elgar, 2008.

Shavinina, Larisa V. "Understanding Innovation: Introduction to Some Important Issues." In *The International Handbook on Innovation*, edited by Larisa Shavinina, 3–16. Kidlington, Oxford: Elsevier Science Ltd, 2003.

Swede, George. "Poetic Innovation." In *The International Handbook on Innovation*, edited by Larisa Shavinina, 471–84. Oxford, UK: Elsevier Science Ltd, 2003.

Varpio, Laura, Paradis, Elise, Uijtdehaage, Sebastian, and Young, Meredith. "The Distinctions Between Theory, Theoretical Framework, and Conceptual Framework." *Academic Medicine* 95, no. 7 (2020): 989–94. 10.1097/ACM.0000000000003075

Zhao, Fang. "Exploring the Synergy between Entrepreneurship and Innovation." *International Journal of Entrepreneurial Behaviour & Research* 11, no. 1 (2005): 25–41. 10.1108/13552550510580825

# 2 Key Terms for Mutual Understanding

To guide theory development, I used a purposive literature review, diverse case studies in art history, reflections on personal observations, and the grounded theory method. In discussing the grounded theory method, John Creswell states, "a key idea is that theory development does not come off the shelf, but rather is generated or grounded in data from participants who have experienced the process."[1] Continuing, Creswell suggests that by discovering emerging patterns in the data, the researcher is able to "generate a general explanation (a theory) of a process, an action, or an interaction shaped by the views of a large number of participants."[2] Long recognised as an effective scientific method by researchers in the qualitative paradigm, the grounded theory method is a systematic process with defining features; such as a focus on a process or action that has distinct steps or phases, data collection by way of connecting implicit meanings, and data analysis leading to either a general theoretical model or a theory presented as a diagram, propositions, or a discussion.[3] Prior to presenting three formal theories in discussion formats, it is important to make sure that the key terms I use in these discussions are clearly defined.

## Defining art history and the arts

When most people think of **art history**, they may think of the historical study of the visual arts. However, it is important to note that all references to art history in this book are references to *the broader historical study of the visual, literary, and performing arts*. In addition, all references to **the arts** are broader references to *the expressive visual, literary, and performing art forms that incorporate skill or imagination in the creation of esthetic objects, environments, or experiences that can be shared with others*. In both the sociology of the arts literature and art history literature, scholars often refer to the primary practitioners

DOI: 10.4324/9781003142393-2

of the arts as **artists**; or individuals who are "... skilled in the practice of an **art form** (i.e., *a form of artistic expression*) in which creative activity is dependent upon aesthetic judgment, imagination and originality."[4]

## Defining art worlds and their guiding conventions

In this book, a reference to **art worlds** is a reference to diverse sociocultural networks in which members work together to co-produce endorsed forms of art. Sociologist Howard Becker defines an art world as "... *the network of people whose cooperative activity organized via their joint knowledge of conventional means of doing things, produces the kinds of artworks that the art world is noted for.*"[5] As a practical example, there is a local network of people who work together to co-produce country music in Nashville, Tennessee; or as some sociologists might say, there is an art world in Nashville, Tennessee, that co-produces country music.[6] Alternatively, sometimes it is helpful to think of an art world as *all the people who work together to co-produce an endorsed form of art in a particular society.* Using this logic, an art world could develop anywhere in a society or be embedded in any community. In cases where this is true, there may be one or more art worlds embedded within suburban communities and one or more art worlds embedded within inner-city communities. There may be art world members who identify as artists, creatives, arts managers or administrators, and art world members who identify as black, white, biracial, multiracial, children, teenagers, adults, male, female, heterosexual, non-binary, and/or LGBTQ+. In addition, members of art worlds often establish business arrangements with dealers, sellers and presenters in order to distribute endorsed forms of art to collectors, customers and audiences, make a profit, and sustain co-production. While these business arrangements are sometimes initiated or enabled by entrepreneurs, philanthropy or cultural policies, the sustainability of an art world depends largely upon the collective decisions and co-operative actions of all of their members.[7]

Although Pierre Bourdieu's related concept of an *art field* rightly draws our attention to how collective decision-making power is structured and distributed in art worlds,[8] I've chosen to use Becker's concept of an art world to encourage readers to think about how innovation in the arts changes the cooperative behavior and business arrangements of art world members. In support of this choice, Becker states, "... the metaphor of world – which does not seem to be at all true of the metaphor of field – contains people, all sorts of people, who are in the middle of doing something that requires them to pay attention to each other, to take account consciously of the existence of others and to shape what they do in light of what others do."[9] In addition, Becker's concept of an art world helps us to recognise that the production of endorsed forms of art is a collective activity carried out by both artists and support personnel (e.g., arts administrators), rather than an individual activity carried out by an artist. Importantly, Becker's concept also helps us to understand that artworks produced by art world members "... are not the products of individual makers," but are joint products created by groups of people who follow *conventions* (i.e., *patterns, rules of order, standard ways of doing things*).[10] According to Becker, conventions in art worlds guide the co-production of endorsed forms of art by dictating the form in which creative materials will be combined, suggesting the appropriate way an endorsed form of art should be practiced, and by regulating the relations between artists and audiences.[11]

## Defining arts-based products

A *product* can be defined as *something that is manufactured or refined for sale.* From the perspective of those who sell artworks to consumers, consumers of art share a need or desire for *arts-based products, or objects and experiences associated with endorsed forms of art.* Although social perceptions of art change over time, generally in order for consumers of art to recognise an arts-based product, the product must be tangible, visible, and/or audible in nature. In addition, the product must be perceived by the consumer to be a form of art endorsed by members of an art world. Some examples of arts-based products that fit these criteria include a sculpture, a dramatic play, an art exhibition, a salsa dance performance, a song, a photograph, or a dramatic film.

Richard Caves' research on creative industries suggests that arts-based products are creative products of infinite variety.[12] Ever considered how many different forms of classical dance exist in the world (e.g., Odissi Dance, European Ballet, Indigenous Hoop Dance)? How about all the different categories of music available to the listener on the music streaming platform Spotify?[13] Even if you attend the live production of a play for two consecutive nights, the performing arts experience will be different in some way on the second night because it is impossible for humans to replicate that exact same experience while performing live.

From customers' perspective, products of infinite variety may present a challenge. With so many arts-based product variations to choose from, it can be difficult for the customer to determine which one(s) they want to buy or buy access to. As Caves notes, while discussing creative industries, "Two songs, two paintings, two action movies may be quite similar in character and quality that consumers see in them, but they are not identical."[14] To help customers make purchasing decisions, dealers, sellers and presenters often group arts-based products into categories called *genres*, which help customers identify arts-based products with similar characteristics, and help art world members differentiate between endorsed art forms. Some examples of genres in the arts include still life painting, jazz dance, fiction, nerdcore hip hop, and Chinese opera.

## Differentiating between arts and non-arts-based products

Arguably, arts-based products are unique from non-arts-based products because – even if an arts-based product is considered by a customer to be useless, or considered to be of little to no economic value, the customer may still desire it. For example, compared to a refrigerator, a painting is a different type of product. At the end of the day, if the customer cannot use the refrigerator to achieve the manufacturer's intended purpose (i.e., to keep items cold), the customer is unlikely to buy the refrigerator because the product is not useful. Alternatively, a painting may have been created by the maker with no intended function or use at all. The maker may have been an infant, random object, computer-based artificial intelligence, or wild animal. Nevertheless, the painting may still be in demand because the customer's perceived value of the painting is not primarily based on what the customer can use the painting to do, but rather based on who the maker of the painting is, what the painting makes the customer think about, and/or how the painting makes the customer feel.

## Defining innovation

It's no secret that innovation and entrepreneurship are often perceived as complementary practices. However, research suggests that compared to those who study entrepreneurship, there are relatively few individuals around the world who specifically study innovation.[15] Those who do contribute to the innovation literature from across a wide variety of academic disciplines. While many scholars agree that innovation is beneficial for society, there is little to no consensus amongst innovation scholars on a general definition. This lack of consensus has not stopped scholars from proposing definitions.

For example, the internationally renowned economist Joseph Schumpeter (1934) defined **innovation** as "*the practical implementation of ideas that result in the introduction of new goods or services, or improvement in offering goods or services.*"[16] In discussing innovation in the sciences, Robert Brown defines innovation as "... *a subset of creativity that involves the creation of a new idea, but also involves its implementation, adoption and transfer.*"[17] Contributors to *The International Handbook on Innovation* offer readers a wide range of scholarly perspectives on "... what innovation is, how it is developed, how it is managed, how it is assessed, and how it affects individuals, groups, organisations, societies, and the world as a whole."[18] Given the diversity of scholarly perspectives, it seems that a general definition of innovation is difficult to advance because, just like the arts, innovation is a multi-dimensional concept.

Building consensus on a general definition is also challenging because the concept of innovation can change based upon the prefix you attach to it. The addition of a prefix tends to refer to a unique type of innovation or point readers to a specific dimension of innovation. For example, whereas technology innovation can refer to the introduction or implementation of a new technology that satisfies an unmet need, scholars suggest that *social innovation* can refer to (1) societal transformation, (2) a model of organisational management, (3) social entrepreneurship, (4) the development of new products, services, and programs, and (5) a model of governance, empowerment, and capacity building.[19] When discussing theories of innovation, Henrik Berglund makes us aware of common conceptual problems.[20] For example, many people believe that innovation is a type of change, but as Berglund points out, not all change is innovative.[21] Also, many people believe that innovation is a process, but as Berglund points out, innovation can also be an outcome.[22] Moreover, the concept of innovation is shaped by the **innovation context**, or *the time period, situation, and/or environment whereby one or more innovation efforts take place.*

For example, based on Kenneth Khan's observations, innovation processes in business industries generally require one or more people to (1) identify an opportunity for product innovation, (2) develop the innovative product, (3) introduce the innovative product to a **market** (i.e., *a group of consumers who share the same consumer preferences*), (3) deliver the innovative product to consumers, and (4) gain market acceptance.[23] However, after observing innovation processes in art worlds, Becker describes the innovation process differently. To Becker, innovation processes carried out by art world members involve "winning organisational victories, succeeding in creating around one-self the apparatus of an art world, mobilising enough people to co-operate in regular ways that sustain and further their idea."[24] As you can see, both the prefix and the context of innovation can influence how we define and frame the concept of innovation.

Although innovation is highly sought after in many societies, success tends to be elusive because people tend to believe that innovation has to be something new, complex in design, broad in scope, and revolutionary. However, according to Peter Drucker's observations, when something is truly considered to be an innovation in society, it tends to be something that is not necessarily new, "breathtakingly simple" (e.g., why didn't I think of that?), focused in scope, and feasible.[25] It tends to be an idea that originates from an unexpected success or failure, a discrepancy between what a situation is and what it should be (i.e., an incongruity), the recognition of a process need, a change in industry or market structure, a demographic shift in the population, changes in perception, or the acquisition of new knowledge.[26] It also tends to be something that members of a particular *industry* (i.e., *group of businesses that work together in an economy to profit from the production and distribution of similar products and services*) were previously unaware of, and something that requires those who plan to sell the innovation to create a new category of classification in order to more accurately describe the innovation's value to potential stakeholders, customers and/or consumers.

## Differences between innovation and invention

Although innovation may at times require *invention* (i.e., *creating or introducing something new for the first time*), it is important to note that innovation always requires more than invention. As Kahn notes, "Innovation is more than ideas and creating something new; execution in terms of getting the innovation in the hands of consumers, having purposeful use, and achieving market acceptance is an essential part of innovation."[27] While the terms invention and innovation may seem at times to be interchangeable, one key thing to remember is that although some inventions are *innovative* (i.e., *possessing the potential to result in innovation*), not all inventions result in innovation.

For example, in 1910, watching a film in a fully lit auditorium was considered by some to be an innovative way of reducing audience members' eye fatigue. Support for this idea led to the invention of a new cinematic experience called *the daylight motion picture*. However, this invention did not result in innovation in the 19th-century motion picture industry because as Phil Edwards notes, "... well-lit movie theatres lacked the quality picture found in a dark theater."[28] Heidi Neck, Christopher Neck, and Emma Murray extend our understanding of the differences between invention and innovation when they state, "Innovations and inventions are often paired together, but the difference lies in demand."[29] Perhaps, this is why most inventions are not recognised as innovations because although they may be considered by the inventor(s) to be innovative, many inventions lack evidence of market demand and diffusion.

**Defining diffusion**

It is important to note that the systematic process of innovation does not end after an innovative product, process or service has been created. Innovative products, processes, and services need to be introduced and shared amongst potential stakeholders, customers and consumers in order to have any chance of being widely accepted, adopted, or utilised. Innovation scholars like Everett Rodgers call this part of the systematic process of innovation *diffusion*; a concept that has been advanced by many innovation scholars around the world. In the book *Diffusion of Innovations,* Rodgers defines diffusion as "*a process in which an innovation is communicated through certain channels over time among the members of a social system.*"[30] Based on Rodgers' research, diffusion happens when an innovator introduces an innovation, when public opinion of the innovation changes from unfavorable to favorable, and when customers start to believe that the innovation is valuable to them. While diffusion is a necessary part of all innovation processes, some strategy is required because the diffusion of innovations is full of uncertainty, and thus can result in swift and widespread rejection instead of adoption.[31]

**Defining adoption**

Rodgers' research suggests that the systematic process of innovation does not end after diffusion. Innovative products, processes, and services still need to be widely adopted in order to result in the outcome of innovation. In theory, without widespread adoption, innovative processes, products, and services will be rejected, ignored, or considered irrelevant by most people. Rodgers' findings help us to understand that innovations are adopted by different groups of people at different rates.[32] In addition, Rodgers' findings suggest that the adoption of an innovation is a decision-based process occurring in multiple stages.[33] To help us better understand that process for different groups of adopters, Rodgers identifies shared characteristics of these groups and classifies them as innovators, early adopters, early majority, late majority, and laggards.[34]

As Rodgers notes, *"the relative speed with which an innovation is adopted by members of a social system"* is generally recognised in the innovation literature as **the rate of adoption**.[35] Generally, adoption occurs on an individual level when a person puts the innovative process, product, or service into use for the first time and then seeks positive re-enforcement from others on that decision. However, as Rodgers notes, "Getting a new idea adopted, even when it has obvious advantages, is difficult. Many innovations require a lengthy period of many years from the time when they become available to the time when they are widely adopted."[36] In cases where this is true, innovators may seek out best practices and strategies for speeding up the rate of adoption.

### Innovation and innovators: Selected definitions

To reiterate, there is no consensus amongst innovation scholars on a general definition of innovation. Arguably, there is far more agreement amongst innovation scholars as to what core processes are necessary for the systematic process of innovation (i.e., (re)introduction, diffusion, adoption). If one chooses to follow this logic, then one might recognise *the facilitators of these three core processes* as **innovators**.

Notably, there is some discourse amongst innovation scholars concerning whether adoption is the most appropriate word to describe the final core process. As Berglund references, some innovation scholars have even suggested swapping the word "adoption" with the word "accepted" or "implemented" or "utilised."[37] Given that the innovation context often guides these semantic decisions, I've selected definitions that will help clarify concepts of innovation in the arts.

### Conclusions: So what is innovation in the arts?

Broadly defined, innovation in the arts is a unique concept of innovation. A **concept** is *a notion or image that comes to mind when one thinks of a related observation or idea*. For example, in the book *International Entrepreneurship in the Arts*, Lidia Varbanova suggests that arts and cultural organisations tend to think of the concept of innovation in one of the following ways; "... creating ideas and transforming them into goods or services that have value for audiences," "developing new approaches that are an alternative to creative production," "creating and implementing new or enhanced products, services or processes in the arts" and "finding new ways to make artistic products, venues or organisations self-sustainable by implementing new methods and exploring resources."[38] Obviously, there are a wide variety of ways to think about the concept of innovation in the arts. As such, it is important to clarify these concepts of interest by offering clear and concise definitions, and by identifying specific outcome indicators which will help you evidence each concept. The three concepts of innovation in the arts discussed in this book are:

- **Art Innovation**, or *the creation, diffusion, and widespread endorsement of a new form of art in an art world.* In theory, the outcome of art innovation is evidenced by widespread social and institutional endorsement of a new form of art by art world members.
- **Art Movement Innovation**, or *the introduction, diffusion, and widespread acceptance of a guiding ideology for a new art movement.* In theory, the outcome of art movement innovation is evidenced by the formation of a collective artistic identity in an art world along with new communal and associative relationships between members of the art movement.
- **Audience Experience Innovation**, or *the development, diffusion, and widespread integration of a structured experience design for visual, literary or performing arts audiences.* In theory, the outcome of audience experience innovation is evidenced by an increasing number of arts administrators integrating the experience design into their presenting arts organisation(s), and/or using it as a guide for arts presenting.

It is important to recognise that these three concepts are not necessarily new, only narrowed in scope in order to increase the clarity of the type of innovation in the arts I'm referring to. For example, in considering *innovation in the arts,* Varbanova references one type when framing *innovation as art form development.*[39] Plausibly, just like music innovation and poetic innovation, there are multiple types of innovation(s) in the arts.[40] However, without greater clarity of the specific type, clarity of the innovation context, and outcome indicators evidencing the concept, you may be confused about which type of innovation in the arts, I'm talking about.

Before reading further, please note that each of the formal theories presented in this book was written in a way so that they can be understood independently of each other. As such, feel free to read out of sequence if so desired. Those interested in a specific theory should skip to the theory of interest specified below:

Chapter 3: A Theory of Art Innovation
Chapter 4: A Theory of Art Movement Innovation
Chapter 5: A Theory of Audience Experience Innovation

## Notes

1  John W. Creswell, *Qualitative Inquiry & Research Design: Choosing Among Five Approaches*, Kindle (3r (Thousand Oaks, CA: Sage Publications, 2013), chap. 4.
2  Creswell, chap. 4.
3  Juliet Corbin and Anselm L. Strauss, *Basics of Qualitative Research: Techniques and Procedures for Developing Grounded Theory*, 3rd ed. (Thousand Oaks, CA: Sage Publications, 2008); Creswell, *Qualitative Inquiry & Research Design: Choosing Among Five Approaches.*
4  Dagobert D. Runes and Harry G. Schrickel, eds., *Encyclopedia of the Arts* (Philosophical Library, 1946), 70.
5  Howard S. Becker, *Art Worlds*, 25th Anniversary (Berkeley, CA: University of California Press, 2008), x.
6  George H. Lewis, "The Creation of Popular Music: A Comparison of the 'Art Worlds' of American Country Music and British Punk," *International Review of the Aesthetics and Sociology of Music* 19, no. 1 (1988): 35–51, https://doi.org/10.2307/836444.
7  Howard S. Becker, "Art as Collective Action," *American Sociological Review* 39, no. 6 (1974): 767–76.
8  Pierre Bourdieu, *The Rules of Art: Genesis and Structure of the Literary Field* (Stanford, CA: Stanford University Press, 1996).
9  Becker, *Art Worlds*, 375.
10  Becker, 35.
11  Becker, "Art as Collective Action."
12  Richard Caves, *Creative Industries* (Cambridge, MA: Harvard University Press, 2000).
13  Glenn McDonald, "Every Noise at Once," Every Noise at Once, N/A, https://everynoise.com/.
14  Caves, *Creative Industries*, 6.
15  Larisa V. Shavinina, "Understanding Innovation: Introduction to Some Important Issues," in *The International Handbook on Innovation* (Kidlington, Oxford: Elsevier Science Ltd, 2003), 3–16.
16  Joseph A. Schumpeter, "The Theory of Economic Development: An Inquiry into Profits, Capital, Credit, Interest, and the Business Cycle" (Chicago, IL: University of Illinois at Urban-Champaign's Academy for Entrepreneurial Leadership Historical Reference in Entrepreneurship, 1934), https://ssrn.com/abstract=1496199.
17  Robert W. Brown, "Embracing Entrepreneurship Across Disciplines," in *Embracing Entrepreneurship Across Disciplines* (Cheltenham, UK: Edward Elgar Publishing, 2015), 41.

18  Larisa V. Shavinina, *The International Handbook on Innovation* (Kidlington, Oxford: Elsevier Science Ltd, 2003), xxvii.
19  Julie Caulier-Grice et al., "Defining Social Innovation," White Paper (The Young Foundation, 2012), 6, https://youngfoundation.org/wp-content/uploads/2012/12/TEPSIE.D1.1.Report.DefiningSocialInnovation.Part-1-defining-social-innovation.pdf.
20  Henrik Berglund, "Interesting Theories of Innovation: The Practical Use of the Particular" (Chalmers University of Technology, 2004), https://citeseerx.ist.psu.edu/viewdoc/download?doi=10.1.1.201.8112&rep=rep1&type=pdf.
21  Henrik Berglund.
22  Henrik Berglund.
23  Kenneth B. Kahn, "Understanding Innovation," *Business Horizons* 61, no. 3 (2018): 453–60.
24  Becker, *Art Worlds*, 301.
25  Peter Drucker, *Innovation and Entrepreneurship: Practice and Principles* (New York, NY: Harper & Row, 1985), 135–37.
26  Drucker, *Innovation and Entrepreneurship: Practice and Principles.*
27  Kenneth B. Kahn, "Understanding Innovation," 457.
28  Phil Edwards, "These 7 Inventions Were Supposed to Change the World. They Failed. Badly.," vox.com, February 26, 2021, https://www.vox.com/2015/2/26/8114391/inventions-dumb-fads.
29  Heidi M. Neck, Christopher P. Neck, and Emma L. Murray, *Entrepreneurship: The Practice and the Mindset*, Kindle (Thousand Oaks, CA: Sage, 2018), sec. 7743.
30  Everett M. Rodgers, *Diffusion of Innovations*, 5th, Kindle ed. (New York, NY: Free Press, 2003), sec. 783.
31  Everett M. Rodgers, sec. 1062.
32  Everett M. Rodgers, *Diffusion of Innovations.*
33  Everett M. Rodgers, chap. 5.
34  Everett M. Rodgers, 279.
35  Everett M. Rodgers, sec. 1116.
36  Everett M. Rodgers, *Diffusion of Innovations.*
37  Henrik Berglund, "Interesting Theories of Innovation: The Practical Use of the Particular."
38  Lidia Varbanova, *International Entrepreneurship in the Arts*, Kindle (NY, NY: Routledge, 2017), 77.
39  Varbanova, 69.
40  George Swede, "Poetic Innovation," in *The International Handbook on Innovation* (Oxford, UK: Elsevier Science Ltd, 2003), 471–84.

## References

Becker, Howard S. "Art as Collective Action." *American Sociological Review* 39, no. 6 (1974): 767–76.
Becker, Howard S. *Art Worlds.* 25th Anniversary. Berkeley, CA: University of California Press, 2008.

Berglund, Henrik. "Interesting Theories of Innovation: The Practical Use of the Particular." Chalmers University of Technology, 2004. https://citeseerx. ist.psu.edu/viewdoc/download?doi=10.1.1.201.8112&rep=rep1&type=pdf

Bourdieu, Pierre. *The Rules of Art: Genesis and Structure of the Literary Field.* Stanford, CA: Stanford University Press, 1996.

Brown, Robert W. "Embracing Entrepreneurship Across Disciplines." In *Embracing Entrepreneurship Across Disciplines*, 31–50. Cheltenham, UK: Edward Elgar Publishing, 2015.

Caulier-Grice, Julie, Davies, Anna, Patrick, Robert, and Norman, Will. "Defining Social Innovation." White Paper. The Young Foundation, 2012. https:// youngfoundation.org/wp-content/uploads/2012/12/TEPSIE.D1.1.Report.Defining SocialInnovation.Part-1-defining-social-innovation.pdf

Caves, Richard. *Creative Industries.* Cambridge, MA: Harvard University Press, 2000.

Corbin, Juliet, and Anselm L. Strauss. *Basics of Qualitative Research: Techniques and Procedures for Developing Grounded Theory.* 3rd ed. Thousand Oaks, CA: Sage Publications, 2008.

Creswell, John W. *Qualitative Inquiry & Research Design: Choosing Among Five Approaches.* Kindle (3r. Thousand Oaks, CA: Sage Publications, 2013.

Drucker, Peter. *Innovation and Entrepreneurship: Practice and Principles.* New York, NY: Harper & Row, 1985.

Edwards, Phil. "These 7 Inventions Were Supposed to Change the World. They Failed. Badly." vox.com, February 26, 2021. https://www.vox.com/ 2015/2/26/8114391/inventions-dumb-fads

Kahn, Kenneth B. "Understanding Innovation." *Business Horizons* 61, no. 3 (2018): 453–460.

Lewis, George H. "The Creation of Popular Music: A Comparison of the 'Art Worlds' of American Country Music and British Punk." *International Review of the Aesthetics and Sociology of Music* 19, no. 1 (1988): 35–51. 10.2307/836444.

McDonald, Glenn. "Every Noise at Once." *Every Noise at Once*, N/A. https:// everynoise.com/.

Neck, Heidi M., Christopher P. Neck, and Emma L. Murray. *Entrepreneurship: The Practice and the Mindset.* Kindle. Thousand Oaks, CA: Sage, 2018.

Rodgers, Everett M. *Diffusion of Innovations.* 5th, Kindle ed. New York, NY: Free Press, 2003.

Runes, Dagobert D., and Schrickel, Harry G., eds. *Encyclopedia of the Arts.* Philosophical Library, 1946.

Schumpeter, Joseph A. "The Theory of Economic Development: An Inquiry into Profits, Capital, Credit, Interest, and the Business Cycle." Chicago, IL: University of Illinois at Urban-Champaign's Academy for Entrepreneurial Leadership Historical Reference in Entrepreneurship, 1934. https://ssrn. com/abstract=1496199

Shavinina, Larisa V. *The International Handbook on Innovation*. Kidlington, Oxford: Elsevier Science Ltd, 2003.

Shavinina, Larisa V. "Understanding Innovation: Introduction to Some Important Issues." In *The International Handbook on Innovation*, edited by Larisa V. Shavinina, 3–16. Kidlington, Oxford: Elsevier Science Ltd, 2003.

Swede, George. "Poetic Innovation." In *The International Handbook on Innovation*, edited by Larisa V. Shavinina, 471–84. Oxford, UK: Elsevier Science Ltd, 2003.

Varbanova, Lidia. *International Entrepreneurship in the Arts*. Kindle. NY: Routledge, 2017.

# 3 A Theory of Art Innovation

## Theory

Arguably, one way to achieve innovation in the arts is to pursue art innovation. In theory, **art innovation** is *the creation, diffusion, and widespread endorsement of a new form of art in an art world*. This type of innovation occurs when the innovator focuses on an endorsed form of art, identifies conventions that guide practitioners, adds new guiding conventions, presents the resulting work publicly, and provokes discourse in the hopes of convincing opinion leaders in an art world to endorse the resulting work as a new form of art. As more and more opinion leaders engage in the discourse, knowledge and awareness of the new combination of conventions increases, and some begin to recognise the resulting work's unique possibilities for artistic expression. With sustained discourse, curiosity amongst art world members increases, provoking some to become early endorsers by being amongst the first to imitate the innovator's creative process, or by signaling social or institutional endorsement.

## Theoretical framework

Support for this theory aligns with Everett Rodgers' definition of innovation as *"an idea, practice, or object that is perceived as new by an individual or other unit of adoption."*[1] In Rodgers' view, "It matters little, so far as human behavior is concerned, whether or not an idea is objectively new as measured by the lapse of time since its first use or discovery. The perceived newness of the idea for the individual determines his or her reaction to it. If an idea seems new to the individual, it is an innovation."[2] Conceptually, Rodgers' view of innovation can help us to recognise newly endorsed forms of art as art innovations. What follows is a defensible rationale for this assertion.

DOI: 10.4324/9781003142393-3

After all, throughout art history, newly endorsed forms of art have originated from new ideas (e.g., the idea to paint with oil). Newly endorsed forms of art have been defined as new artistic practices (e.g., the practice of oil painting). Newly endorsed forms of art have also been recognised as new objects (e.g., a new painting made with oil). Art has also been recognised in a wide variety of forms. In the 1946 *Encyclopedia of the Arts*, editors Runes & Schrickel define the word *form* as *a mode of arranging or coordinating the factors in a work of art*.[3] Guided by Rodger's view of innovation, it is plausible that there are at least some people who might think of a newly endorsed form of art as an innovation or *a newly endorsed way of arranging or coordinating the factors in a work of art*.

For example, in the book *Innovators in Sculpture*, Dianne Durante states, "The innovations we're looking at in Innovators in Sculpture are not novelty for the sake of novelty (e.g., the emergence of life-size sculptures). Every one of them gave its creator more power to make you stop, look and think. And these innovations were not gimmicks or minor tweaks. They were so useful that they allowed many other sculptors to convey their values and ideas more effectively."[4] In *The Classical Music Book*, contributing authors reference *Ars Nova*, a new polyphonic sound hailed in the 14th century as *the new art*.[5] Recently published books like *Art Quilts Unfolding: 50 Years of Innovation*, *Blues Legacy: Tradition and Innovation in Chicago*, *Music of the First Nations: Tradition and Innovation in Native North America*, *Judson: Innovation in Stained Glass*, and *Shibori: The Inventive Art of Japanese Shaped Resist Dying* not only support the concept of art innovation but also serve as an indicator that the art innovation literature is expanding.

## Where do new art forms come from?

In the 21st century alone, new and emerging art forms like Sci-Art, Artificial Intelligence (AI) Art, Kinetic Poetry, Grime Music, and Hiplet Dance have emerged from art worlds around the world. Based on Runes and Schrickel's definition of *form, art forms* seem to be the preferred means by which artists express themselves and communicate their ideas to others.[6] Given the evidence of new and emerging art forms, one wonders where artists get their ideas for these new means of creative expression and communication?

Sociologist Victoria Alexander provides some insight when positing that "All new forms evolve out of established ones."[7] For example, research suggests that there are many art forms that include some of the conventional practices of older art forms. Country music includes conventional practices derived from the performance of English ballads, Celtic and Irish fiddling, and jazz and blues music.[8] Tap dance includes conventional practices derived from both African and Irish American dances.[9] Opera includes conventional practices derived from Greek storytelling.[10] As noted by Barbara Hanning in the Encyclopedia Britannica:[11]

> The collaborators of the first operas (in the early 17th century) believed they were creating a new genre in which music and poetry, in order to serve the drama, were fused into an inseparable whole, a language that was in a class of its own—midway between speaking and singing.

Such research findings and case studies in art history support the position that newer art forms evolve out of older art forms. If this is true, then Becker's observations of conventions in art worlds may help to explain where art innovators get ideas for new art forms. For example, in the sociology of the arts literature, the word *genre* is often used by scholars to reference a particular category of art; or perhaps more specifically, "a form of art that shares a set of conventions."[12] Becker likens these conventions to patterns, norms, and standard ways of doing things in art worlds.[13] In his empirical study of artist networks, one conclusion Becker reached was that "People who produce a work of art usually do not decide things afresh. Instead, they rely on earlier agreements now become customary, agreements that have become part of the conventional way of doing things in that art."[14] Becker's observations suggest that conventions make the co-production of a particular genre of art easier and less costly because most art world members already know the conventional way(s) of co-producing in that genre.

Interestingly, one key difference between the older and newer art forms of reference is that the newer forms include some conventions of the older. For example, when discussing innovators in music, Becker references the stories of Harry Partch and John Cage, whom, "... for all their innovations, retained many conventions of the music world."[15] Additionally, Becker has observed groups of art world members, whom, " ... orient themselves to the world of canonical and conventional art" and whom " ... change some of its conventions and more or less unwittingly accept the rest."[16] Continuing, Becker observes that "The work of these innovators is often incorporated into the historical corpus of the established art world, whose members find the innovations useful in producing the variation required to rescue art from ritual."[17] Thus, as Becker suggests, "Every art work creates a world in some respects unique, a combination of vast amounts of conventional materials *with some that are innovative.*"[18]

## Who are the art innovators?

While conventions in art worlds make co-production easier and less costly, Becker's observations suggest that those same conventions may stifle art innovation by dictating which materials should be combined to create an endorsed form of art, and by signaling the appropriate way(s) in which an endorsed form of art should be co-produced by art world members and (re)presented to audiences.[19] Despite the known innovation constraints imposed by conventions, when it comes to creating a new artwork, Alexander has observed that "Most artists follow conventions in most aspects of their work."[20]

However, as Ellen Winner has observed, some artists " ... intentionally set out to confuse us about our definition of art, to make us question our definition, and to make us expand our definition."[21] Diana Crane has observed that some artists " ... have a strong commitment to iconoclastic aesthetic values."[22] Becker has observed that some artists find the conventions in art worlds unacceptably constraining, and " ... propose innovations the art world refuses to accept as within the limits of what it ordinarily produces."[23] Continuing Becker states, "Instead of giving up and returning to more acceptable materials and styles ..." these aspiring art innovators " ... continue to pursue the innovation without the support of other art world personnel."[24] Arguably, in doing so, these aspiring art innovators take on the reputation risks of creating a new form of art, diffusing a new form of art, and encouraging widespread endorsement of a new form of art in an art world.[25]

## What are the known risks of pursuing art innovation?

Becker's observations of the behavior of a specific group of art world members he calls *Mavericks* suggests that artists may take on various types of risk when pursuing art innovation, including a risk to their own reputation in one or more art worlds.[26] First, by deviating from guiding conventions, aspiring art innovators begin a creative process with greater uncertainty of the resulting work. To help make this point, consider if I asked you to create a finger painting. You probably already know how to create that form of art because the guiding conventions are widely known. However, consider if I asked you to create a new form of finger painting. In theory, this task would be more difficult than the former because there are no guiding conventions for that creative process.

Second, because art innovators' creative process deviates from convention, it's likely the resulting work will be perceived as unfamiliar to most art world members. Art is socially constructed and discourse about art shapes and influences how people define art in a society. In cases where this is true, the resulting work may not be recognised as art, a work of art or a form of art at all. Further, creative processes provide no absolute guarantee that the resulting work will be recognised as art by art world members. Consider the famous art history case associated with the creative work entitled *Fountain*, in which one of the now most famous conceptual artworks was unanimously rejected as art by a jury.[27] As Becker notes, " ... not everything can be made into a work of art just by definition or the creation of consensus, for not everything will pass muster under currently accepted art world standards."[28] In art worlds, the creative work and the artwork may be related concepts, but they are not always perceived by art world members to be the same thing.

Third, while the introduction of a new art form may result in widespread endorsement amongst members of an art world, it may also result in widespread rejection, which could damage the aspiring innovator's reputation in one or more art worlds.[29,30] For example, Barnett Newman is recognised in art history as a pioneering artist of abstract expressionism. Pablo Picasso is recognised as a pioneering artist of cubism, and Andy Warhol is recognised as a pioneering artist of pop art. It is worth noting that upon introduction, the innovative creative works of all of these pioneering artists were heavily criticised and rejected as art by certain art world members.

## Who legitimises new art forms?

In cases where the general public relies on members of art worlds to help them determine what art is, proposed new forms of art will not be recognised by the general public as legitimate without the endorsement of certain art world members. Endorsement is generally defined as the act of giving one's public approval or support to someone or something. Arguably, social endorsement plays an important role in art innovation processes because art is socially constructed, and newly introduced and/or proposed art forms require some form of social endorsement in order to gain legitimacy as art in a given society. As

Shyon Baumann notes when discussing a general theory of artistic legitimation, numerous studies help to explain how expressive practices and creative works gained social endorsement.[31] Referencing *Rap* as one example, Baumann notes:

> The legitimacy of rap music when it was first created was quite low, for example, especially among white, middle-class audiences. Rap's legitimacy has steadily increased so that now it now enjoys recognition as a legitimate popular art. This recognition reflects a fairly wide, though by no means absolute, consensus that the justifications for rap as art are valid. That is to say, the justifications are found by various audiences to be convincing arguments for the case for rap to be popular art. Should the art world for rap make claims that rap is a legitimate high art form, it remains to be seen how successful such claims would be.[32]

Just like Baumann, Rodgers also draws our attention to the social endorsement of art when discussing how Rap music was adopted by White Americans.[33] As another example, consider that at present, most self-identified poets probably know what a Haiku poem is, in part because most of them have endorsed the idea that *Haiku poetry* is a legitimate form of poetry. In cases where this is true, it evidences the social endorsement of a form of art. Alternatively, at present, most self-identified poets probably do not know what *Tritriplicata poetry* is, likely because this new and emerging form of poetry created by Arjun Tupan has not yet received much social endorsement throughout the broader literary world.[34] Given this example, I assume that social endorsement plays an important role in art innovation processes, in part because social endorsement increases what Everett calls the *rate of adoption*, or "the relative speed with which an innovation is adopted by members of a social system."[35]

Additionally, George Dickie's (1974) *Institutional Theory of Art* helps us to understand how some art institutions might enable any creative work to be widely considered a legitimate form of art.[36] As Stephen Davies references, "Institutional accounts hold that something is a work of art as a result of its being honored, dubbed, or baptized, as such by someone who is authorized thereby to make it an artwork in consequence of her or his position within the informal institution of the artworld."[37] Where this is true, some arts-based institutions may have the ability to enable any creative work to suddenly be eligible for presentation by performing arts organisations, exhibition by museums and galleries, preservation by arts or cultural policy,

and/or funding by arts-granting organisations. Based on contemporary examples of the institutional theory of art occurring as
Dickie theorised (i.e., Barney Smith's Toilet Seat Art Museum,
Museum of Broken Relationships, The New York Earth Room),[38] I
assume that institutional endorsement plays an important role in art
innovation processes, in part because this form of endorsement not
only increases what Everett calls the *rate of adoption* but also provides
art innovators with access to infrastructural support.[39]

Despite the effect that social and institutional endorsement can have
on the legitimacy of art, it is important to note that social and institutional endorsement requires consensus only somewhere, not ev-
erywhere.[40] Thus, a new art form does not need social endorsement
from all art world members, or endorsement from all art(s) institutions
in order to gain legitimacy. Arguably, what a new art form needs most
is an endorsement from one or more opinion leaders in art worlds who
the general public likes, knows, and trusts. As a practical example,
you're probably more likely to believe that Jazz Opera is a new art
form if Miles Davis says it is. If one recognises Miles Davis as a world-
famous jazz musician, then they will probably trust Davis' opinion
over someone who is not a world-famous jazz musician, or someone
who is not a member of an art world that co-produces jazz music.
Becker provides insight into this scenario when he states:

> A relevant feature of organized art worlds is that, however their
> position is justified, some people are more commonly seen by
> many or most interested parties as more entitled to speak on
> behalf of the art world than others; the entitlement stems from
> them being recognized by the other participants in the cooperative
> activities through which that world's works are produced and
> consumed as the people entitled to do that.[41]

> Whether other art world members accept them as capable of
> deciding what art is because they have more experience, because
> they have an innate gift for recognizing art, or simply because they
> are, after all, the people in charge of such things and therefore
> ought to know – whatever the reason, what lets them make the
> distinction and make it stick is that the other participants agree
> that they should be allowed to do it.[42]

Sometimes, the general public may also rely on the endorsements of
cultural intermediaries to help them to determine the legitimacy of new
art forms. Although there are many proposed definitions, you might

want to think of cultural intermediaries as taste-makers who " ... leverage their own experience into occupational resources to legitimate certain forms of culture over others."[43] For example, Isadora Duncan is often recognised in art history as one of the pioneers of modern dance. Based on Isadora Duncan's autobiography *My Life*, upon recognising the celebrated actress Mrs. Patrick Campbell's endorsement, social elites in 20th-century London started perceiving Duncan's unique style of dance as a legitimate art form.[44] Plausibly, widespread endorsement of Duncan's unique style as a form of art might have never happened if those social elites had not trusted the opinion of Mrs. Patrick Campbell. With this understanding, trusted opinion leaders' endorsements may be another useful form of social endorsement for art innovators, because the endorsements of cultural intermediaries can influence perceptions of art outside of an art world.

## What is the process of creating a new art form?

Creation is innately innovative or capable of resulting in innovation. However, to create a new form of art with the intention of art innovation, one assumption is that the art innovator(s) engage(s) in iterative rounds of creative experimentation with the intention of creating a new combination of conventions for guiding artistic practice. As a practical example, the innovator might begin by choosing ballet. Then, by identifying the conventions which guide ballet dancers, and then by experimenting with different combinations of ballet conventions and the guiding conventions of other art forms.

For example, instead of dancing on pointe (one convention in ballet), the innovator might try to dance in gym shoes. In addition to the Plié (bending of the knee or knees), Relevé (to raise), Pirouette (a complete turn of the body on one foot, on point or demi-pointe), and the Grande Jeté (a big jump from one foot to the other); the innovator might also integrate salsa turns like closed holds, open holds, crossed holds and change of hand holds. The result would be a recombination of the conventions (hereafter referred to as a new combination) which guides both ballet and salsa dancers, and a different form of both ballet and salsa dance.

As another example, the art innovator might begin by (1) focusing on Opera singing, (2) identifying certain conventions which guide Opera singers, (3) adding one or more unconventional practices (e.g., singing in a punk rock style), testing and (re)adjusting the creative process according to what they learn, until finally recognising a new combination that allows Opera singers to express themselves, in a form that has not been previously realised. You might call this new combination Punk Rock Opera singing.[45]

## Diffusing the art innovation

Next, the innovator attempts to diffuse knowledge and awareness of the new combination throughout an art world. Rodgers defines diffusion as *the process by which an innovation is communicated through certain channels over time among members of a social system.*[46] Contextually, aspiring art innovators might facilitate the diffusion of this new combination in many ways, such as by sharing the idea with a targeted group of artists, educating a group of art world members about the new combination, or presenting this new combination to an audience. Rodgers might refer to all these efforts as demonstrations that have the potential to increase the observability of the innovation.[47]

Given the innovator's unconventional creative process, the new combination might be recognised as *avant-garde* by some art world members; a historic reference to an artist's realisation of a new or unusual experimental idea. Nevertheless, the innovator will attempt to diffuse the innovation because diffusion is a necessary activity for gaining social and/or institutional endorsement for a new form of art. As art is socially constructed, social endorsements will likely be made collectively by groups of art world members; or as Rodgers suggests, by way of consensus among members of a social system.[48] As some art institutions can be independent social systems of their own, institutional endorsements may likely be determined by arts administrator(s) with the authority to make endorsement decisions for those institutions.[49] However, it is important to note that institutional endorsement of a new combination is risky for art institutions because it could have a negative effect on the reputation of the art institution.

While some art world members will accept the new combination as a new form of art, Mukti Khaire's research suggests that some will not without first engaging in discourse about it. After all, the innovator's creative process is unconventional. The defining elements of the resulting work are unfamiliar. The new combination may result in an artistic practice that is radically different from those known to most art world members. For all these reasons, some art world members may be suspicious and hesitant to provide an endorsement. As Khaire notes when discussing the unique nature of the creative industries:

> Because artists seek to push boundaries, new categories of cultural goods are quite often radically different from existing categories,

rather than being incremental improvements on the goods already available. Moreover art serves to make the unimagined and unknown seem possible, plausible and known. When artists employ their creativity to achieve this goal in a work, the resulting product often pushes against prevailing beliefs and cultural values, inciting suspicion and hostility.[50]

Based on Khaire's findings, the problem here is obvious. The new combination has not been socially or institutionally endorsed yet as a form of art. Arguably, a new combination is more likely to be endorsed by art world members when its defining characteristics are perceived as similar to those of a widely endorsed art form.[51] In cases where this is true, the innovator might choose to refer to the new combination as a blend between a well-known art form and a newer one. As a practical example, instead of calling a blend between salsa conventions and ballet conventions *Torkasa dance*, the innovator might refer to the new combination as *Salett dance or Ballesa dance.* This play on words roots the newer art form to an older art form that has already been widely endorsed, thus directing art world members to conventions that many already perceive as art. Another problem is that upon initial introduction, most art world members will not know how to evaluate the quality of the new combination in practice because there will be no existing criteria for evaluating its quality. As a practical example, at present, could you distinguish between high-quality Ballesa dance and low-quality Ballesa dance?

In summary, the unconventional creative process, the obscureness of the resulting work, and the absence of an existing criteria for evaluating the quality of practice will likely contribute to psychological barriers to art innovation endorsement. As Khaire notes on the topic, " … radically new works of art cannot be assessed and valued using existing conceptions and norms of value; rather new criteria and conventions of value are needed."[52] Given psychological barriers to art innovation endorsement, most art world members will rely on discourse about the new combination to determine whether the new combination should be endorsed as a new form of art.

## Known strategies for speeding up the rate of endorsement

Recognising some art world members' resistance to endorsement, the innovator may seek the help of cultural intermediaries and opinion leaders in art worlds to help (re)shape public perceptions and/or help to improve the rate of endorsement in an art world. As Rodgers notes on the topic of the diffusion of innovations, "Change agent's success in securing the adoption of innovations is positively related to the extent that he or she works through opinion leaders."[53] Examples of opinion leaders in art worlds include but are not limited to pioneering artists, entertainment superstars and celebrities, wealthy patrons of arts organisations, art critics, members of visual, literary and performing arts juries, leaders of prominent arts organisations, foundations who fund arts and cultural activities, editors of both academic and commercial arts-based journals, and trusted cultural intermediaries.

One known strategy for speeding up the rate of endorsement in art worlds is to identify existing forums where opinion leaders in art worlds regularly gather, and then introduce the new combination in those forums (e.g., the private *Weird Art Group* on Facebook). Another known strategy is to create a new forum, and then invite or pay opinion leaders to lead discussions about the new combination in that forum (e.g., *Quills Fest* produced by the Oregon Shakespeare Festival). Another strategy is to incite the interest of opinion leaders by publicly challenging one or more opinion leaders' perception of art, presenting the new combination publicly, and by provoking those opinion leaders to respond to the presentation publicly (e.g., Duchamp's *Fountain*).

Whatever the strategy, both working with and inciting opinion leaders in art worlds is risky because opinion leaders have a unique and influential position in art worlds, and because they may be opposed to change.[54] However, as more and more opinion leaders engage in the innovator's desired discourse, curiosity about the new combination will increase, and some art world members will begin to recognise its possibilities for artistic expression. Based on Khaire's research findings, discourse seems to be one of the main tools that art innovators use to sustain the diffusion of art innovations in art worlds. Pragmatically, if no one is talking about, discussing, or debating about the new combination, then it will not gain social or institutional endorsement as a new form of art in an art world. As Khaire notes on the role that discourse plays in cultural industries, "Without intersubjective agreement over the value of the new idea, most consumers, unsure of the social validity of adopting it, will not change their beliefs or preferences."[55] Thus, with sustained discourse about the new combination, curiosity will increase, provoking some art world members to become early endorsers either by being amongst the first to imitate the innovator's creative process or by being amongst the first to signal social or institutional endorsement.

## Conclusion: So what does success look like?

Given research findings on the diffusion of innovations, it is likely that the process of art innovation ends after the new combination is endorsed by some art world members, some art(s) institutions, and some members of the general public as a new form of art. In cases where these milestones occur, I would call it a success, because the innovator has acquired social and institutional endorsement of the new combination. This type of innovation can have a significant impact on both societies and economies because based on Becker's observations, new art worlds develop around such innovations. In cases where this is true, upon conclusion of an art innovation process, the innovator may have laid the foundation for the development of a whole new art world, new arts-based industry, and/or new economy of culture.[56]

Over time, some early endorsers may become recognised in art history as pioneers of a new art form, largely because they will be amongst the first to both endorse the new art form and imitate the innovator's creative process before others. As these pioneering artists demonstrate the new art form to art world members in their own social networks, the diffusion process will change from being centralised to decentralised. With this change, the diffusion of the art innovation will now branch throughout multiple social networks, extending far beyond the innovator's initial diffusion capabilities.[57]

## Case studies of art innovation

### Modern Dance

One case of art innovation can be identified by researching the origins of Modern Dance in Western society. Although the concept of Modern Dance was influenced by pioneers in European eurythmics (i.e., harmonious bodily movement as a form of artistic expression) and labanotation (i.e., a system of recording human movement), Isadora Duncan (an American dancer) is widely recognised in Western art history as one of the innovators of Modern Dance. The development of Modern Dance was largely motivated by Duncan's passion for dancing, and by Duncan's study of the sculptures of Ancient Greece from which she drew much inspiration. Evidence of Duncan's unconventional style of dance, and her contribution to art history can be identified in the Encyclopedia Britannica:

**Isadora Duncan**, original name (until 1894) **Angela Duncan**, (born May 26, 1877, or May 27, 1878, San Francisco, California, U.S.—died September 14, 1927, Nice, France), American dancer whose teaching and performances helped to free ballet from its conservative restrictions and presaged the development of modern expressive dance. She was among the first to raise interpretive dance to the status of creative art.[58]

In the 20th century, Duncan's unique style of dance stood out in the West because she danced barefoot, and because she embraced a complete freedom of movement. In doing so, Duncan deviated from the guiding conventions of Ballet at the time. Through iterative creative experimentation, Duncan played with the conventions of Ballet until finally recognising a new combination of conventions and a new way to express herself in a form that was previously unrealised.

To facilitate diffusion, Duncan tried performing in her new unique style in Chicago and New York but was met with little success. Frustrated by rejection, Duncan left the United States at the age of 21 in order to seek better luck abroad. One night, while Duncan was dancing in her unique style in a small garden of a tiny house in Kensington Gardens (London), the celebrated English actress Mrs. Patrick Campbell unexpectedly came across and took notice. In Duncan's own words:

> One night, in the Indian summer, Raymond and I were dancing in the gardens, when an extremely beautiful woman in a large black hat appeared and said, "Where on earth did you people come from?" "Not from the earth at all" I replied, "but from the moon." "Well she said, "whether from the earth, or moon, you are very sweet; won't you come and see me?"[59]

According to the Encyclopedia Britannica, "Through the patronage of the celebrated actress Mrs. Patrick Campbell, she (Duncan) was invited to appear at the private receptions of London's leading hostesses, where her dancing, distinguished by a complete freedom of movement, enraptured those who were familiar only with the conventional forms of the ballet, which was then in a period of decay. It was not long before the phenomenon of a young woman dancing barefoot, as scantily clad as a woodland nymph, crowded theatres, and concert halls throughout Europe."[60] This is evidence of the diffusion of an art innovation assisted by a cultural intermediary and opinion leader (Mrs. Patrick Campbell); without Campbell's patronage and social capital, Duncan's unique style may have never been endorsed as a form of art by Western dance audiences or by Western dance artists in the 20th century. As noted in the Encyclopedia Britannica:

> Certainly her place as a great innovator in dance is secure: Her (Duncan's) repudiation of artificial technical restrictions and reliance on the grace of natural movement helped to liberate the dance from its dependence on rigid formulas and on displays of brilliant but empty technical virtuosity, paving the way for the later acceptance of modern dance as it was developed by Mary Wigman, Martha Graham, and others.[61]

## Conceptual Art

Another famous case of art innovation involves the "readymade" artwork titled *Fountain* submitted in 1917 to the Society of Independent Artists (SIA) salon. The salon was a visual art exhibition that included a juried art competition. At the time (1917), SIA claimed that *they would accept any work of art* into the salon if the artist paid the application fee. Although there is debate in art history about who submitted Fountain for consideration (commonly believed to be either Marcel Duchamp or Elsa von Freytag-Loringhoven),[62] it is important to note that the submission was essentially a porcelain urinal turned on its side, signed and dated, "R. Mutt, 1917."[63] Guided by sacred aesthetic beliefs, SIA rejected this submission on the grounds that *it was not a true work of art*. Duchamp, who was a member of the Board of Directors himself, resigned from the Board in protest, openly challenging the logic and basis of the salon committee's decision.

To facilitate the diffusion of this new combination, Duchamp intentionally provoked public discourse about the incident through the publication of an article in the journal *The Blind Man* (issue #2). The name of the published article was *The Richard Mutt Case*.[64] In support of Duchamp's position that *Fountain* should be recognised as a work of art, Beatrice Wood (a friend of Duchamp) wrote, "Whether Mr. Mutt with his own hands made the fountain or not is of no importance. He chose it. He took an ordinary article of life, placed it so that its useful significance disappeared under the new title and point of view, created a thought for the object."[65] This is evidence of diffusion assisted by an opinion leader (i.e., Beatrice Wood). This is also evidence of the successful diffusion of an art innovation, as sustained peer discourse on this incident increased the rate of endorsement over time. Eventually, widespread endorsement of *Fountain* as a new form of art expanded public perceptions of what visual art could be in the West, leading to what most visual artists now recognise as the birth of *conceptual art*. Notably, in 2004, *Fountain* was recognised in a survey of over 500 art experts as "The world's most influential piece of modern art."[66]

### Turntablism

Turntablism is the artistic practice of using turntables, a cross fader, records and great timing to create new music, sound effects, mixes, and beats. DJ (i.e., disc jockey) Theodore Livingston (a.k.a. Grand Wizard Theodore) is widely credited by hip-hop historians as a turntable pioneer, and the inventor of *the scratching technique*, which is now widely recognised in hip-hop history as one of the defining conventions of Turntable practice. For readers who are not hip-hop fans or turntable practitioners, *scratching* references the sound intentionally made when a phonograph disc record is rubbed back and forth on the turntable. In 1975, Livingston discovered the scratching technique by accident while DJ'ing at his home in the Bronx, New York. In Livingston's own words:

> I used to come home from school and go in my room and practice a lot, and this particular day I came home and played my music too loud, and my mom was banging on the door and when she opened the door, I turned the music down but the music was still playing in my headphones, and she was screaming, 'If you don't turn the music down you better turn it off' and I had turned down the speakers but I was still holding the record and moving it back and forth listening in my headphones, and I thought, 'This really sounded something ... interjecting another record with another record.' And as time went by, I experimented with it trying other records and soon it became scratching.[67]

While many DJs had already been matching beats and extending the break-down parts of songs thanks to turntable pioneers like DJ Cool Herc and DJ Grandmaster Flash, Livingston's DJ technique was unconventional because it consisted of lifting the stylus out of the entrenched path of the groove, dropping it down on other parts of the record, shifting its direction back and forth, slowing down its motion and speeding it up. Livingston's technique was considered innovative because it resulted in a new type of rhythmic sound previously unrealised.

Livingston diffused his new style of DJ'ing by incorporating the scratching technique into his performances at public parks and local parties. By observing Livingston's technique during these performances, DJs could hear how this new technique expanded the expressive capacity of their turntables. Recognising the possibilities for artistic expression, many DJs began to imitate Livingston's style, and incorporate scratching into their own performances. As the rate of endorsement increased over time, new and emerging hip-hop audiences began to recognise Livingston's technique as a new form of hip-hop music.[68]

## Chinese Opera

The classical Peking Opera (Ching-Hsi) in China (also known as *Chinese Opera or The Classical Theatre of the Chinese*) is a form of musical theatre that dates back to the Qing Dynasty (1644–1911). At present, Chinese Opera consists of over 100 different styles. However, attendance and participation rates have been in steady decline in China since the late 20th century. For example, in 1997 Henry Chu reported in the LA Times that, "Peking Opera is fast disappearing from the stages it once ruled throughout China. Its audience is dropping by as much as 5% a year by one estimate. If the trend continues, experts fear, one of the world's great art forms for two centuries is in danger of vanishing within a generation."[69] The death of Chinese Opera (i.e., no practitioners, no presentations) would be culturally significant given that the artform survived the Japanese occupation in the 1930s and a ban on traditional performances during the 1960s Cultural Revolution in China. In 1994, Sheila Teft provided insight on some of the external factors which have contributed to the gradual decline of Chinese Opera's attendance and participation rates:

> Great opera houses are being torn down or converted into discos, karaoke clubs and movie theaters. Performing standards are dropping and opera troupes, financially strained and in disarray, rely more and more on tourist audiences and overseas performances to survive. Actors and teachers, working for almost the same pay today as when the opera was highly popular 40 years ago, are lured away by the bigger salaries of business or movie companies, and the once extensive national network of rigorous training schools is shrinking. Peking Opera is not as popular now, so students don't have as much of a sense of devotion. Some students think that if they go into another career, they won't have to work so hard," says Ma Mingjun, an opera performer and teacher at the Beijing Middle School.[70]

At present (21st century), many Peking Opera (feeder) schools are still in decline, further contributing to a labor pipeline problem for the Chinese Opera industry.[71] Motivated by cultural policies and widespread changes in the Chinese Opera industry, art innovators started making changes to the conventions which guide practice, resulting in a new form of Chinese Opera referred to as "New Opera" or "Revolutionary Opera."[72] According to Jiang Yimin (Professor at the Peking University Academy of Opera), whereas older forms of Chinese Opera use traditional Chinese singing styles, New Opera, " ... combines Western compositional structures with Chinese singing."[73] According to Yimin, these changes were first recognised in 1945 and first demonstrated through a production called *The White Haired Girl*.[74]

Despite the new combination, Chinese Opera as a whole is still experiencing a decline in attendance and participation rates in the 21st century; in part because Chinese Opera is still not attracting young students and younger audiences. In addition, Chinese opera is still largely unfamiliar to most Western opera audiences. More recently, aspiring art innovators such as Yimin have attempted to make Chinese Opera more familiar and relatable to Western audiences by incorporating the *Italian Bel Canto style of singing*. As Yimin notes, "By incorporating Chinese pronunciation into the singing style to create *China Bel Canto*, we have had more success."[75] Continuing, Yimin notes, "In July, the troupe traveled to the Chinese embassy in London to perform this mixed genre, singing Chinese folk songs and even Western-style bel canto as part of a revolutionary opera. The performance was a resounding success, primarily because the audience understood the story and found it engaging."[76] However, as Yimin notes:

> Chinese opera still strives to become a key player on the global stage rather than remaining a side act for small audiences. The prerequisite for this, however, is erasing regional or ethnic barriers to understanding. We need to encourage greater cross-cultural exchange, in part by letting go of the desire to faithfully adhere to impenetrable original pieces. Only by broadening our appeal in this way will Chinese opera take its place alongside existing Western forms.[77]

## Notes

1  Everett M. Rodgers, *Diffusion of Innovations*, 5th, Kindle ed. (New York: Free Press, 2003), 12.
2  Everett M. Rodgers, 12.

3 Dagobert D. Runes and Harry G. Schrickel, eds., *Encyclopedia of the Arts* (Philosophical Library, 1946), 360.
4 Dianne L. Durante, *Innovators in Sculpture*, Kindle (Dianne L. Durante, 2020), 9.
5 *The Classical Music Book* (New York: DK Publishing, 2018), 15.
6 Dagobert D. Runes and Harry G. Schrickel, *Encyclopedia of the Arts*, 360.
7 Victoria D. Alexander, *Sociology of the Arts: Exploring Fine and Popular Forms* (Malden, MA: Blackwell, 2003), 74.
8 Sara Egge, "The Origins of Country Music," March 19, 2017, https://nortoncenter.com/2017/03/19/the-origins-of-country-music/.
9 "From Margins to Mainstream: A Brief Tap Dance History," University of Michigan, June 21, 2019, https://ums.org/2019/06/21/from-margins-to-mainstream-tap-dance-history/.
10 Michael Ewans, "Greek Drama in Opera," in *A Handbook to the Reception of Greek Drama* (West Sussex, UK: John Wiley & Sons, 2016), 464–85.
11 Barbara R. Hanning, "Opera," Britannica, 2007, https://www.britannica.com/art/opera-music.
12 Alexander, *Sociology of the Arts: Exploring Fine and Popular Forms*, 73.
13 Howard S. Becker, *Art Worlds*, 25th Anniversary (Berkeley, CA: University of California Press, 2008), 35.
14 Howard S. Becker, "Art as Collective Action," *American Sociological Review* 39, no. 6 (1974): 770.
15 Becker, *Art Worlds*, 244.
16 Becker, 244.
17 Becker, 244.
18 Becker, 63.
19 Becker, "Art as Collective Action."
20 Alexander, *Sociology of the Arts: Exploring Fine and Popular Forms*, 73.
21 Ellen Winner, *How Art Works* (New York: Oxford University Press, 2019), 26.
22 Diana Crane, *The Transformation of the Avant-Garde: The New York Art World, 1940–1985* (Chicago, IL: Unversity of Chicago Press, 1989), 1.
23 Becker, *Art Worlds*, 233.
24 Becker, 233.
25 Alexander, *Sociology of the Arts: Exploring Fine and Popular Forms*, 145.
26 Becker, *Art Worlds*, chap. 8.
27 Jon Mann, "How Duchamp's Urinal Changed Art Forever," Artsy.net, 2017, https://www.artsy.net/article/artsy-editorial-duchamps-urinal-changed-art-forever.
28 Becker, *Art Worlds*, 155.
29 Becker, chap. 11.
30 Alexander, *Sociology of the Arts: Exploring Fine and Popular Forms*, 145–47.
31 Shyon Baumann, "A General Theory of Artistic Legitimation: How Art Worlds Are like Social Movements," *Poetics* 35, no. 1 (2007): 50.
32 Shyon Baumann, 49.
33 Everett M. Rodgers, *Diffusion of Innovations*, 220–21.
34 Arjan Tupan, "What Is That Tritriplicata Thing?," *Tripple Effect* (blog), June 11, 2020, https://medium.com/the-tripple-effect/what-is-that-tritriplicata-thing-866ccea7fba9.
35 Everett M. Rodgers, *Diffusion of Innovations*, 221.

36  George Dickie, "What Is Art? An Institutional Analysis," in *Aesthetics: A Comprehensive Anthology* (Hoboken, NJ: Wiley Blackwell, 1974), 449–60.
37  Stephen Davies, "Defining Art and Artworlds," *Journal of Aesthetics and Art Criticism* 73, no. 4 (2015): 382, https://doi.org/10.1111/jaac.12222.
38  Jordanna Lippe, "Eight of the Strangest Art Museums Around the World," *Travel + Leisure*, 2016, https://www.travelandleisure.com/attractions/museums-galleries/unusual-art-museums.
39  Margaret Jane Wyszomirski, "Support for the Arts: A Four-Part Model," *Journal of Arts Management, Law, and Society* 32, no. 3 (2002): 222–41, https://doi.org/10.1080/10632920209596976.
40  Shyon Baumann, "A General Theory of Artistic Legitimation: How Art Worlds Are like Social Movements," 49–50.
41  Becker, *Art Worlds*, 151.
42  Becker, 151.
43  Giannina Warren and Keith Dinnie, "Cultural Intermediaries in Place Branding: Who Are They and How Do They Construct Legitimacy for Their Work and for Themselves?," *Tourism Management* 66, no. 1 (2017): 303, https://doi.org/10.1016/j.tourman.2017.12.012; Pierre Bouraieu, *Distinction: A Social Critique of the Judgement of Taste* (Cambridge, MA: Harvard University Press, 1984).
44  Isadora Duncan, *My Life* (Boni and Liveright, 1927).
45  Treble Staff, "10 Essential Punk Rock Operas," 2015, https://www.treblezine.com/24712-10-essential-punk-rock-operas/.
46  Everett M. Rodgers, *Diffusion of Innovations*, 35.
47  Everett M. Rodgers, 389.
48  Everett M. Rodgers, 28.
49  Everett M. Rodgers, 28–29.
50  Mukti Khaire, *Culture and Commerce: The Value of Entrepreneurship in Creative Industries*, Kindle (Stanford, CA: Stanford University Press, 2017), chap. 1, sec 8, para 2.
51  Otto G. Ocvirk et al., *Art Fundamentals: Theory and Practice*, 12th ed. (New York, NY: McGraw-Hill, 2013), 11.
52  Khaire, *Culture and Commerce: The Value of Entrepreneurship in Creative Industries*, chap. 1, section 7, para 2.
53  Everett M. Rodgers, *Diffusion of Innovations*, 388.
54  Everett M. Rodgers, 27.
55  Khaire, *Culture and Commerce: The Value of Entrepreneurship in Creative Industries*, chap. 2, sec 3, para 7.
56  Becker, *Art Worlds*, 310.
57  Everett M. Rodgers, *Diffusion of Innovations*, 397.
58  The Editors of Encyclopedia Britannica, "Isadora Duncan."
59  Isadora Duncan, *My Life*, 47.
60  The Editors of Encyclopaedia Britannica, "Isadora Duncan."
61  The Editors of Encyclopedia Britannica, "Isadora Duncan."
62  Julian Spalding and Glyn Thompson, "Did Marcel Duchamp Steal Elsa's Urinal?," *The Art Newspaper*, 2014, https://www.theartnewspaper.com/2014/11/01/did-marcel-duchamp-steal-elsas-urinal.
63  Mann, "How Duchamp's Urinal Changed Art Forever."
64  Bowdoin College Museum of Art, "A Fascinating 'Fountain' and 'The Blind Man' (Nos. 1 and 2) Enter the BCMA Collection," *Art Museum*,

December 21, 2020, https://www.bowdoin.edu/art-museum/news/2020/blind-man-duchamp.html.

65 Mann, "How Duchamp's Urinal Changed Art Forever."
66 Charlotte Higgins, "The Most Influential Piece of Modern Art," *Salon*, December 4, 2004, https://www.salon.com/2004/12/02/top_10_artworks/.
67 Jason Lee Oakes, "Grand Wizard Theodore's Turntables: Smithsonian Year of Music Object of the Day, August 13."
68 "The Art of Turntablism," History Detectives: Special Investigations, 2014, https://www.pbs.org/opb/historydetectives/feature/the-art-of-turntablism/.
69 Henry Chu, "An Old Art Struggles in New China," *Los Angeles Times*, 1997, https://www.latimes.com/archives/la-xpm-1997-05-23-mn-61647-story.html#:$\sim$:text=Ravaged by the 1966–76,a year by one estimate.
70 Sheila Teft, "China Loses Its Passion for the Peking Opera - a National Treasure," *The Christian Science Monitor*, 1994, https://www.csmonitor.com/1994/1102/02101.html?cmpid=mkt:ggl:dsa-np&gclid=CjwKCAjwqvyFBhB7EiwAER786UYQhwAjmodLTP8-o4Bmax6nhCxXBlI6wLoCezeLWZMSC2607rcPKBoC2QQQAvD_BwE.
71 Qi Xijia, "Shanghai School of Peking Opera Experiencing Tragic Decrease in Performers and Audiences," *Global Times*, 2017, https://www.globaltimes.cn/content/1032196.shtml.
72 Jiang Yimin, "Should Chinese Opera Westernize to Find Global Audience?," *The Theatre Times*, 2017, https://thetheatretimes.com/chinese-opera-westernize-find-global-audience/.
73 Jiang Yimin.
74 Jiang Yimin.
75 Jiang Yimin.
76 Jiang Yimin.
77 Jiang Yimin.

## References

Alexander, Victoria D. *Sociology of the Arts: Exploring Fine and Popular Forms.* Malden, MA: Blackwell, 2003.

Baumann, Shyon. "A General Theory of Artistic Legitimation: How Art Worlds Are like Social Movements." *Poetics* 35, no. 1 (2007): 47–65.

Becker, Howard S. "Art as Collective Action." *American Sociological Review* 39, no. 6 (1974): 767–76.

Becker, Howard S. *Art Worlds.* 25th Anniversary. Berkeley, CA: University of California Press, 2008.

Bourdieu, Pierre. *Distinction: A Social Critique of the Judgement of Taste.* Cambridge, MA: Harvard University Press, 1984.

Bowdoin College Museum of Art. "A Fascinating 'Fountain' and 'The Blind Man' (Nos. 1 and 2) Enter the BCMA Collection." *Art Museum*, December 21, 2020. https://www.bowdoin.edu/art-museum/news/2020/blind-man-duchamp.html

Chu, Henry. "An Old Art Struggles in New China." *Los Angeles Times*, 1997. https://www.latimes.com/archives/la-xpm-1997-05-23-mn-61647-story.html#:$\sim$:text=Ravaged by the 1966-76,a year by one estimate.

Crane, Diana. *The Transformation of the Avant-Garde: The New York Art World, 1940–1985.* Chicago, IL: University of Chicago Press, 1989.

Davies, Stephen. "Defining Art and Artworlds." *Journal of Aesthetics and Art Criticism* 73, no. 4 (2015): 375–84. 10.1111/jaac.12222.

Dickie, George. "What Is Art? An Institutional Analysis." In *Aesthetics: A Comprehensive Anthology*, edited by Steven M. Cahn, Stephanie Ross, and Sandra Shapshay, 449–60. Hoboken, NJ: Wiley Blackwell, 1974.

Duncan, Isadora. *My Life.* Boni and Liveright, 1927.

Durante, Dianne L. *Innovators in Sculpture.* Kindle. Dianne L. Durante, 2020.

Egge, Sara. "The Origins of Country Music," March 19, 2017. https://nortoncenter.com/2017/03/19/the-origins-of-country-music/.

Ewans, Michael. "Greek Drama in Opera." In *A Handbook to the Reception of Greek Drama*, edited by Betine van Zyl Smit, 464–85. West Sussex, UK: John Wiley & Sons, 2016.

Hanning, Barbara R. "Opera." *Britannica*, 2007. https://www.britannica.com/art/opera-music.

Higgins, Charlotte. "The Most Influential Piece of Modern Art." *Salon*, December 4, 2004. https://www.salon.com/2004/12/02/top_10_artworks/.

History Detectives: Special Investigations. "The Art of Turntablism," 2014. https://www.pbs.org/opb/historydetectives/feature/the-art-of-turntablism/.

Khaire, Mukti. *Culture and Commerce: The Value of Entrepreneurship in Creative Industries.* Kindle. Stanford, CA: Stanford University Press, 2017.

Lippe, Jordanna. "Eight of the Strangest Art Museums Around the World." *Travel + Leisure*, 2016. https://www.travelandleisure.com/attractions/museums-galleries/unusual-art-museums.

Mann, Jon. "How Duchamp's Urinal Changed Art Forever." *Artsy.net*, 2017. https://www.artsy.net/article/artsy-editorial-duchamps-urinal-changed-art-forever.

Oakes, Jason Lee. "Grand Wizard Theodore's Turntables: Smithsonian Year of Music Object of the Day, August 13." *Smithsonian Music* (blog), 2019. https://music.si.edu/story/grand-wizzard-theodores-turntables-smithsonian-year-music-object-day-august-13.

Ocvirk, Otto G., Robert E. Stinson, Philip R. Wigg, Robert O. Bone, and David L. Cayton. *Art Fundamentals: Theory and Practice.* 12th ed. New York: McGraw-Hill, 2013.

Rodgers, Everett M. *Diffusion of Innovations.* 5th, Kindle ed. New York: Free Press, 2003.

Runes, Dagobert D., and Harry G. Schrickel, eds. *Encyclopedia of the Arts.* Philosophical Library, 1946.

Sarasvathy, Saras D. *Effectuation: Elements of Entrepreneurial Expertise.* Cheltenham, UK: Edward Elgar, 2008.

Spalding, Julian, and Glyn Thompson. "Did Marcel Duchamp Steal Elsa's Urinal?" *The Art Newspaper*, 2014. https://www.theartnewspaper.com/2014/11/01/did-marcel-duchamp-steal-elsas-urinal.

Teft, Sheila. "China Loses Its Passion for the Peking Opera – A National Treasure." *The Christian Science Monitor*, 1994. https://www.csmonitor.

com/1994/1102/02101.html?cmpid=mkt:ggl:dsa-np&gclid=CjwKCAjwqvy
FBhB7EiwAER786UYQhwAjmodLTP8-o4Bmax6nhCxXBlI6wLoCeze
LWZMSC2607rcPKBoC2QQQAvD_BwE.

*The Classical Music Book*. New York, NY: DK Publishing, 2018.

The Editors of Encyclopaedia Britannica. "Isadora Duncan." *Encyclopaedia Britannica*, September 10, 2021. https://www.britannica.com/biography/Isadora-Duncan

Treble Staff. "10 Essential Punk Rock Operas," 2015. https://www.treblezine.com/24712-10-essential-punk-rock-operas/

Tupan, Arjan. "What Is That Tritriplicata Thing?" *Tripple Effect* (blog), June 11, 2020. https://medium.com/the-tripple-effect/what-is-that-tritriplicata-thing-866ccea7fba9.

University of Michigan. "From Margins to Mainstream: A Brief Tap Dance History," June 21, 2019. https://ums.org/2019/06/21/from-margins-to-mainstream-tap-dance-history/

Warren, Giannina, and Keith Dinnie. "Cultural Intermediaries in Place Branding: Who Are They and How Do They Construct Legitimacy for Their Work and for Themselves?" *Tourism Management* 66, no. 1 (2017): 302–14. 10.1016/j.tourman.2017.12.012.

Winner, Ellen. *How Art Works*. New York: Oxford University Press, 2019.

Wyszomirski, Margaret Jane. "Support for the Arts: A Four-Part Model." *Journal of Arts Management, Law, and Society* 32, no. 3 (2002): 222–41. 10.1080/10632920209596976.

Xijia, Qi. "Shanghai School of Peking Opera Experiencing Tragic Decrease in Performers and Audiences." *Global Times*, 2017. https://www.globaltimes.cn/content/1032196.shtml

Yimin, Jiang. "Should Chinese Opera Westernize to Find Global Audience?" *The Theatre Times*, 2017. https://thetheatretimes.com/chinese-opera-westernize-find-global-audience/

# 4  A Theory of Art Movement Innovation

## Theory

Arguably, one way to achieve innovation in the arts is to pursue art movement innovation. In theory, **art movement innovation** is *the introduction, diffusion, and widespread acceptance of a guiding ideology for a new art movement*. This type of innovation occurs when the aspiring innovator(s) introduces a guiding ideology into an art world that provokes, compels, or motivates a group of art world members to pursue shared artistic goals. As more and more members accept the innovator's guiding ideology, they join the movement by contributing needed resources and/or by participating in collective action with other members of the movement. With sustained participation, this new art movement results in social innovation by way of the formation of a collective artistic identity in an art world, and new communal and associative relationships between members of the art movement.

## Theoretical framework

In theory, an **art movement** is *a social movement led by one or more art world members towards the pursuit of shared artistic goals*. An art movement is recognised as a social movement because it is a "persistent and organised effort involving the mobilisation of large numbers of people to work together to either bring about what they believe to be beneficial social change, or resist or reverse what they believe to be harmful social change."[1] Art movements are recognised as social movements because they tend to follow the same life cycle stages as social movements more broadly, such as incipiency, coalescence, institutionalisation, fragmentation, demise, and sometimes ... revival.[2] Art movements also share many of the same characteristics as social movements.

DOI: 10.4324/9781003142393-4

For example, both art and social movements depend upon collective action to mobilise participants, accomplish the shared goals of the movement, and sustain participation.[3] Both art and social movements are populated by people who develop and share a collective identity.[4] As Rhys Williams states when discussing culture and social movements, " ... movements must create and sustain a collective identity as part of maintaining collective action. That is, people must feel that they share important characteristics with others in the movement, and that this identity is important enough to promote or protect through movement involvement."[5] Continuing, Williams states, "The creation and nurturance of a shared collective identity produces a sense of we-ness in such a way that it can become the basis for action."[6] As more and more artists join and participate in an art movement, art world members will begin to recognise that distinct group association and collective identity in an art world.[7,8,9]

For example, whereas the 20th-century art movement known as Suprematism was an organised effort by a group of Soviet artists to make art without representational form, the 20th-century art movement known as Soviet Constructivism was an organised counter-movement to Suprematism; largely because members of the Soviet Constructivist movement believed that art should be representational and have a direct impact on society.[10] Thus, in the minds of participants in the Soviet Constructivist art movement, Suprematism was harmful to society and not beneficial for social change in the Soviet Union.

Throughout art history, art movements have tended to occur when an innovator intentionally provokes, compels, or motivates other artists to join an **artist collective** or *initiative whereby participating artists agree to work together towards the pursuit of shared artistic goals.* With sustained participation, some art movements have resulted in social innovation by enabling the creation of a new social network amongst artists, and by reconfiguring social relations between art world members.[11] Although art movements tend to begin with an informal organisational structure, such as a quasi-group, they tend to develop over time into formal organisational structures with guiding policies, procedures, and rules of order.[12,13,14]

## What are the benefits of joining art movements?

Research in art history suggests that upon joining an art movement, members may gain new types of social relationships like *communal relations* (i.e., relations based on a mutual feeling of belonging) and *associative relations* (i.e., relations strengthened by rational motives for the relationship). For example, Amy Dempsey's research on 20th-century art movements teaches us that the Impressionist art movement started when a group of artists in Paris got frustrated with the recurrent exclusion of their works from the Official Salons in Paris. Eventually, these young visual artists got together and recognised that they were all experiencing the same problem. To address their shared problem, they decided to organise and host their own public art exhibition. As Dempsey notes, "What united this group of diverse artists was their rejection of the art establishment and its monopoly on what could be exhibited. Towards the end of the 19th century, the Academy was still promoting the ideals of the Renaissance: namely that the subject of Art must be noble or instructive and that the value of a work of Art could be judged by its descriptive likeness to natural objects."[15] From the perspective of these young 20th-century visual artists, the Impressionist art movement provided them with relations with artists who were experiencing the same problem (i.e., communal relations), and relations with artists who had the collective resources to address the problem (i.e., associative relations).

In addition to new types of relations, art movements can sometimes function as creative incubators for artists, as well as peer support groups for aspiring art innovators. In support, sociologist Victoria Alexander points out that avant-garde artists share a desire to create art in a way that no one else has done before, while at the same time "relating to the body of artistic knowledge that already exists."[16] In order to do this, Diana Crane argues "... they need to belong to a social network of other artists who consider aesthetic innovation as their primary goal."[17] Crane's research findings on seven different styles of art suggest that avant-garde artists tend to associate with one another, especially when they participate in the same art movement.[18] Crane's research findings provide empirical evidence that art movements can provide some artists with access to new ideas for artistic creation, along with peer-to-peer encouragement for art innovation. In support of Crane's findings, Alexander posits "networks of avant-garde artists provide the crucible for the sharing of ideas, as well as social support for innovations."[19]

## What is the role of the guiding ideology?

In theorising the process of art movement innovation, sociologist Howard Becker provides insight when recognising that, "... the history of art deals with innovators and innovations that won organizational victories, succeeding in creating around themselves the apparatus of an artworld, mobilising enough people to cooperate in regular ways that sustained and furthered their idea."[20] Notably, there is empirical support in the innovation literature for Becker's observation.

For example, research suggests that some innovations originate from within the individual and are derived from the generation of an idea or series of ideas.[21] Furthermore, the underlying rationale for social movements is always centered around and based on an ideology, or *a combined set of beliefs, ideas, values, principles, ethics, morals, and goals that overlap and form the basis for something.* In discussing the role that ideologies play in the development of social movements, Colin Beck suggests that "Rather than being mere ideas, ideology is distinguished by its active use and its import for shaping and creating certain types of action."[22] Continuing, Beck notes, "... without an ideology that articulates and identifies a mobilization's beliefs or goals it would be difficult to speak of this as a movement at all. Rather, collective action without ideology would appear disorganized and temporary."[23] Operating under the assumption that the cooperative actions undertaken by participants of social movements are at least initially based on the innovator's guiding ideology, it is plausible that cooperative actions undertaken in an art movement are based on a guiding ideology as well. Support for this proposition can be found by reviewing Amy Dempsey's research on the basis of participating in over 100 modern art movements in the 20th century.

For example, *Der Blaue Reiter* (i.e., The Blue Rider) (1911) was an art movement in Germany guided by an ideology that included principles of spiritual mysticism, pantheistic philosophy, and the innovator's passionate belief in the creative expressive freedom of the artist. *Novecento Italiano* (1923) was an art movement in Italy guided by an ideology that included Fascist beliefs and the innovator's aim to revitalise Italian Art. *Concrete Art* (1930) was an art movement in the Netherlands guided by an ideology that included scientific concepts and mathematic principles, as well as the innovator's interest in geometrical abstraction. Clearly, Dempsey's findings show us that art movements are not centered around and based on ideas only, but rather on broader ideologies derived from the innovator's ideas, beliefs, values, principles, ethics, morals, and artistic goals that overlap and form the basis for participation.

### It has to be compelling or inspiring!

Based on Dempsey's findings, it really doesn't seem to matter if the guiding ideology for a new art movement is objectively new. Rather, for the best chance of widespread acceptance, what seems to matter more is the degree to which artists find the guiding ideology compelling and/or inspiring. After all, in order for an art movement to gain participants, the guiding ideology needs to compel or inspire one or more groups of artists in an art world to move towards collective action for as long as the art movement exists.

Bert Klandermans offers some insight when recognising three fundamental reasons why people participate in social movements: "People may want to change their circumstances, they may want to act as members of their group, or they may want to express their views."[24] Continuing, Klandermans recognises that instrumental, identity and ideological motives often combine to influence participation in collective action.[25] Dempsey's research offers supporting evidence, as based on her findings, many artists who participated in the 20th-century modern art movements were motivated to pursue collective action by their (a) shared attitude toward art, (b) shared belief(s) about art, (c) shared desire to reform or revitalise art, (d) shared opposition to another art movement, (e) common interest in artistic experimentation, (f) shared passion for making art in a certain way, (g) common view or perception of art, (h) shared preference for a stylistic practice, (i) common subject matter of interest, and (j) shared interest in promoting a specific social agenda in an art world.[26]

Given these new understandings, the process of art movement innovation may be challenging because the innovator's motives and ideas for collective action might not be shared by particular groups of artists in an art world. Also, guiding ideologies are derived in part from a series of ideas, and *ideas* are *formulated thoughts or opinions* that at times may be difficult to develop and express to certain groups of people. As author John Butman (2013) notes in his book *Breaking Out: How to Build Influence in a World of Competing Ideas,* "It's difficult to develop an idea and harder to express it well. It's tough to get people simply to hear your idea, and harder still to enable them to understand it in ways that come close to your intended meaning."[27]

While some believe that ideation or *the formulation of ideas or concepts* is easier for individuals deemed "creative" in society (e.g., artists, creatives, innovators), ideation can be challenging for anyone because the process requires brainstorming and critical thinking. As such, the development of a compelling ideology for a new art movement will likely require adequate time for brainstorming and critical thinking, and the identification of at least one group of artists who share the innovator's beliefs, values, principles, ethics, and morals. In addition, it will likely require identification of the membership benefit(s) of participating in the new art movement.

## Diffusing the guiding ideology for an art movement

In the innovation literature, diffusion is recognised as "a process in which an innovation is communicated through certain channels over time among the members of a social system."[28] After developing a guiding ideology for a proposed art movement, the innovator facilitates diffusion by sharing the guiding ideology to at least one group of artists in an art world. This diffusion process is risky because the diffusion of innovations is full of uncertainty, and because the introduction of guiding ideologies for shared artistic practice can sometimes result in swift and immediate rejection by art world members.[29] Thus, for the best chance of diffusion, it may be wise to share the guiding ideology within a known network of avant-garde artists; because historically, these types of artists have tended to be early adopters of the guiding ideologies of new art movements, as well as art movement innovators themselves.[30]

## One common strategy for diffusion

While there may be many ways to diffuse a guiding ideology for a new art movement throughout an art world, one way that art movement innovators have done this throughout art history is to *write a manifesto and share it with artists in their social network*. In the art history literature, a *manifesto* is often recognised as *a declarative or persuasive document that communicates and advances a set of aesthetic aims, opinions, views, or plan of action*. As early as the 1880s, visual, literary and performing artists in the West began writing and publishing manifestos; using them to declare shared artistic goals publicly, attract like-minded people, and advocate for widespread changes in diverse art worlds. While some of these manifestos fell on deaf ears (i.e., rejection of the guiding ideology), some successfully compelled and inspired groups of artists to work towards shared artistic goals (i.e., acceptance of the guiding ideology).[31] For reference, an online article by Harriet Baker identifies ten game-changing art manifestos.[32]

It is important to note that all hope is not lost if a published or shared manifesto fails to gain traction or widespread attention in an art world. In theory, if at least one artist perceives a shared manifesto to be compelling, or feels that it is inspirational, it may help the innovator to gain the support of a partner who can help the innovator make the manifesto more compelling or an opinion leader who may come to the innovator's defense during mass rejection. If a large group of artists perceive the revised manifesto to be compelling or inspiring, or an opinion leader manages to change the mindset of those who previously rejected the guiding ideology, it may help the innovator to gain the buy-in or generate the discourse needed to speed up the rate of acceptance.

## Increasing the rate of acceptance

According to Everett Rodgers, **adoption** is *a decision to make full use of an innovation as the best course of action available."*[33] In discussing the adoption process, Rodgers notes, "The decision stage in the innovation-decision process takes place when an individual (or other decision-making unit) engages in activities that lead to a choice to adopt or reject the innovation."[34] For clarity, where applicable hereafter, I will swap the word *adoption* with the word **acceptance**, because people *accept the* guiding ideologies of art movements rather than adopt them. Given this understanding, I assert that after sharing the guiding ideology with artists (diffusion), the innovator must work to increase the rate of acceptance in an art world. To that end, Rodgers points us to five evidenced factors that may influence the rate of acceptance: (a) perceived attributes of the innovation, (b) type of innovation-decision, (c) communication channels, (d) nature of the social system, and (e) the extent of change agents' promotion efforts.[35] While all of these factors have the capability of impacting the rate of acceptance positively and negatively, Rodgers suggests that there are five perceived attributes that can explain about half of the variance in rates of acceptance. Plausibly within the context of art movement innovation, these five perceived attributes may be:

- (relative advantage) the degree to which membership in an art movement is perceived as being more advantageous than membership in another art movement, or not being a member of any art movement
- (compatibility) the degree to which the guiding ideology of an art movement aligns with a particular group of artists' cultural values and beliefs, aligns to guiding ideologies they have previously accepted or is able to meet their current relational needs
- (complexity) the degree to which the guiding ideology of an art movement is perceived as being difficult or hard for artists to understand

- (trialability) the ability of artists to participate in the art movement on their own terms as long as they please
- (observability) the degree to which the collective actions of an art movement are widely observable in an art world

Where these factors of influence are evidenced, to speed up the rate of acceptance, the innovator would be wise to (a) make the guiding ideology easy to understand, (b) share the benefit(s) of joining the art movement broadly, (c) target artists with the same shared values, morals and beliefs, (d) increase public awareness of the art movement, and (e) establish a trial period before asking participants for increased commitment. In doing so, the rate of acceptance will likely increase, compelling more and more artists to accept the innovator's artistic goals as their own goals and to utilise the innovator's ideology as a guide for pursuing those goals with others.

## Delaying the inevitable

No matter the rate of acceptance, all art movements have a life cycle (i.e., beginning, growing participation, peak of participation, decline in participation, dissolution). There is support from scholars across the broader arts literature for this assertion. For example, in discussing the history of modern art, art historian Susie Hodge makes the universal claim that *"All* art movements occur in particular time periods."[36] In discussing the history of aesthetics, scholars Christopher Janaway and Sandra Shapshay (2020) note that "Aestheticism arose out of specific artistic preoccupations in Victorian Britain *[i.e., a time period]*, and is sloganized as the "art for art sake" movement ..."[37] In discussing the Black arts movement that took place in America during the 1960s and 1970s, scholar Johnathan Fenderson states, "... if there is something we can learn from the past, and the Black arts movement more specifically, it is how social movements come to life, wax, wane, and eventually expire."[38]

Research in visual art history suggests that art movements dissolve for a wide variety of reasons. For example, based on Dempsey's research (2010), the Suprematist art movement ended in the 1920s, in part because the Soviet Union ended state support for experimental abstract art.[39] Arguably, this is an example of dissolution brought on by cultural policy. Dempsey's research suggests that the Futurist art movement ended in 1929, primarily because public perceptions of the guiding ideology (e.g., the cult of the machine, the glorification of war) changed over time from favorable to unfavorable. Arguably, this is an example of dissolution brought on by changes in both cultural taste and public perceptions of art.[40,41]

Dempsey's research suggests that *Die Brücke* (The Bridge) art movement ended in 1913, primarily because one leader claimed ownership of the movement, which resulted in a disagreement amongst the movement's participants, which resulted in a formal dissolution of the movement.[42] Arguably, this is an example of dissolution brought on by internal conflict because the actions of one of the leaders served as the catalyst for dissolution. The same could be said for the Orphist art movement, which ended in 1914 primarily because of infighting.[43] In fact, based on a thematic analysis of factors contributing to the dissolution of 100 modern art movements profiled in Dempsey's book, some of the most common were

- The leaders lost interest in pursuing the goals of the art movement
- Public perceptions of the art movement changed from favorable to unfavorable
- Infighting amongst participants of the art movement (including internal disputes over ownership and leadership)
- Organisational fracture of the art movement into different art movements
- Leaders moved to different geographic locations (decentralised leadership)
- Physical death of leaders with no leadership replacement (no leadership transition plan in place)
- Overt government suppression
- War changed members' priorities
- Members were attracted to the guiding ideology of another art movement

## Conclusion: What does success look like?

Given research findings on the diffusion of innovations, it's likely that the process of art movement innovation ends after most members in an art world become aware of the new art movement, or the formation of a new collective artistic identity in that art world. In cases where this milestone occurs, I would call it a success because the innovator has provoked, compelled, and/or motivated a group of art world members to pursue shared artistic goals. This type of social innovation can have a significant impact on a group of art world members because it can provide them with new communal and associative relationships, access to shared collective resources, organised collective power, and the ability to take collective action.

Given the identified reasons why many art movements have dissolved, for the best chance of success, aspiring innovators of art movements may want to consider implementing organisational management strategies to delay the inevitable. Doing so could help extend the life cycle of a new art movement, as well as proactively address many of the known internal conflicts that contribute to their dissolution; many of which might be avoided by way of a co-written mission statement, written co-defined roles and responsibilities of members, at least one revenue-generating income stream to support the goals of the movement, and the creation of a leadership transition plan.

## Case studies of art movement innovation

### *The Dada Art Movement*

Artists Hugo Ball (a writer) and Tristan Tzara (a poet) are widely credited in art history as the founders of the Dada art movement which developed during World War I.[44] The Dada art movement was centered around and based on Ball and Tzara's blended guiding ideologies, which included their shared desire to abandon artistic conventions and shared disdain for the institutional frame of art.[45] As Emily Hage notes when discussing the Dada art movement, "Through their experiments with collage, montage, chance, the ready-made, and the journal medium, the Dadaists – Tzara, Marcel Duchamp, Max Ernst, Hannah Höch, and Dragan Aleksic´, among others – countered deep-seated convictions regarding originality, autonomy, and authenticity; and in defiance of the nationalism that they blamed for the war, they advocated multiplicity."[46]

To facilitate diffusion of the guiding ideology, both Ball and Tzara wrote and published founding manifestos in the form of essays, with Ball publishing in 1916 and Tzara publishing in 1918.[47] Ironically, in Ball's 1916 manifesto, Ball expresses opposition to Dada becoming an art movement; a point of contention that would later contribute to the dissolution of his friendship with Tzara. Seeking to start an art movement, Tzara created and distributed several magazines to diffuse the guiding ideology as well. As Emily Hage notes, "By creating and exchanging magazines such as Dada, as well as Die Schammade, Dada Tank, Der Dada, and dozens more, they forged a sense of identity based on diversity and distance rather than on conformity and proximity. These individuals recognised that the magazine was uniquely suited to fostering connections at a time of censorship as well as restricted travel and exhibition opportunities. They depended upon their graphically stunning publications to learn about each others' artworks and writings and to forge ties with audiences in cities across the globe."[48] As evidenced in art history, both the publication of Ball and Tzara's founding manifestos, and the creation and distribution of Dadist magazines enabled the guiding ideology for the Dada art movement to be diffused within and across diverse art worlds in Western society.[49] Evidence of widespread acceptance can be found throughout the art history literature. For example, Emily Hage notes that "… Dada was a highly influential international movement with advocates in at least ten cities, including Bucharest, Zagreb, Berlin, and New York, by the mid-1920s."[50]

### The New Negro Renaissance Movement

The New Negro Renaissance movement (also sometimes called the Harlem Renaissance) was primarily a 20th-century literary arts movement, as well as a precursor to the Black arts movement of the 1960s. Although the origins of this art movement are disputed, many historians like Jeffrey Stewart consider Dr. Alain LeRoy Locke to be the father of the Harlem Renaissance, which is an indicator of an art movement innovator.[51] According to Stewart's book *The New Negro: The Life of Alain Locke* (2018), the seeds of *The New Negro Renaissance* were planted in 1925, when Locke published a book called *The New Negro: An Interpretation.*

Within this book, Locke introduced a guiding ideology for Black artists and advocated for Black art (e.g., art created by artists who identify as Black, art that expresses Black identity) to be created with a focus on communicating and expressing the beauty of Black people; not as a concession to White power, but to advance the Black community's struggle to express themselves in ways that they (Black people) recognised as beautiful.[52] As Jeffrey C. Stewart notes in his biography, "What was the goal of African American creative expression? Was it to defend Negroes against racism? Or uncover beauty, especially among a people often thought of as lacking in beauty? Later, Locke would discuss these questions in an article entitled *Art or Propaganda?*"[53]

While some Black artists accepted Locke's guiding ideology, some cultural intermediaries were critical and rejected it. For example, scholar and civil rights activist William Edward Burghardt (W.E.B.) Du Bois made his opposition clear when he published a 1926 review of

*The New Negro* in *The Crisis;* an American quarterly magazine founded by Du Bois in 1910, and widely read by Black Americans. In Du Bois's own words[54]:

> Mr. Locke has newly been seized with the idea that Beauty rather than propaganda should be the object of Negro literature and art. His book proves the falseness of his thesis. This is a book filled and bursting with propaganda, but it is propaganda for the most part beautifully and painstakingly done ...
>
> It is the fight for Life and Liberty that is giving birth to Negro literature and art today and when, turning from this fight or ignoring it, the young Negro tries to do pretty things or things that catch the passing fancy of the really unimportant critics and publishers about him, he will find that he has killed the soul of Beauty in his Art.

Du Bois's response draws our attention to the seeds of an alternative guiding ideology for Black artists. Du Bois offered further clarification in a related article published in *The Crisis* that same year named *The Criteria of Negro Art* (1926). In this article, Du Bois famously states:

> Thus all Art is propaganda and ever must be, despite the wailing of the purists. I stand in utter shamelessness and say that whatever art I have for writing has been used always for propaganda for gaining the right of black folk to love and enjoy. I do not care a damn for any art that is not used for propaganda. But I do care when propaganda is confined to one side while the other is stripped and silent.[55]

Essentially, Du Bois believed that 20th-century Black art should be used as an instrumental tool to improve the social conditions of Black people. In addition, Du Bois believed that apolitical Black art was incapable of doing this. As such, Du Bois offered a different ideology for guiding the work of young Black artists in the 20th century; one that was directly opposed to Locke's. In Locke's view, the most productive direction for Black artists in the 20th century was to make art that they felt was beautiful to them. Stewart references Du Bois's passionate opposition when noting that, "Du Bois could no longer suppress his critical feelings and extended his reservations about the philfavor of artistic freedosophy of Beauty in *The New Negro* into a "Symposium" in The Crisis that ran from February to July 1926."[56]

Ironically, Du Bois's thinly veiled attacks and written criticism of Locke's guiding ideology for Black artists ended up compelling and inspiring many young black writers (e.g., Carl Van Vechten, Dubose Hayward, Countee Cullen, Langston Hughes) to engage in the discourse generated by these two scholars; many of whom ended up rejecting Du Bois's guiding ideology in favor of artistic freedom. In support, Stewart notes that "Almost all the younger Negro writers," even those friendly to Du Bois, "... voted for the freedom of the artist and issued a truism: the artist should write what he or she felt."[57]

Up until 1928, Locke never directly addressed any of Du Bois's criticism, perhaps because Du Bois was a revered public figure, an internationally respected African American intellectual, and arguably the leading civil rights spokesman in the United States at the time. However, in 1928 Locke finally addressed Du Bois's criticism directly through the publication of an article entitled *Beauty Instead of Ashes*, and a follow-up article entitled *Art or Propaganda*. In both of these publications, Locke's message to young Black writers was strong and unmistakable, "... move beyond Du Bois, and start thinking and acting like we [Black people] own American literature."[58] Arguably, these dueling article publications written and published from 1925 to 1928 by Du Bois and Locke generated discourse about Black art and served as the catalyst for the development of the New Negro (Harlem) Renaissance movement.

### *De Stijl Movement*

In both the art history literature and the history of graphic design, De Stijl (i.e., translated in English as "The Style") is known as an art movement that developed in the Netherlands in 1917.[59] According to Eskilson's (2019) research, the guiding ideology of De Stijl was co-created by a founding group of artists and architects: namely Theo van Doesburg, Piet Mondrian, Bart van der Leck and Gerrit Rietveld.[60] According to Dempsey, "... the mission of De Stijl was to create a new, international art in the spirit of peace and harmony."[61] Continuing, Dempsey notes, "Van Doesburg, Mondrian, [Georges] Vantongerloo and Van der Leck had already worked together in an attempt to create an abstract visual vocabulary which could be put to practical purposes, and which would communicate their desire for a better society. The use of horizontal and vertical lines, right angles, and rectangular areas of flat colours characterize their work of the period."[62]

To introduce the guiding ideology and facilitate diffusion, Van Doesburg started a journal called *De Stijl* and openly invited visual artists to apply the guiding ideology to graphic and architectural design practice, submit those designs to the journal, and view and discuss those designs together. This particular diffusion strategy seems to have been successful because Van Doesburg published 36 issues in the first three years; and because from 1917 to 1932, the journal established itself as "... a consistent vehicle wherein the ideas of the European avant-garde could be discussed and critiqued."[63] Moreover, "The journal served as a visual example of the group's aesthetic principles in the realm of typography and graphic design."[64] In addition, widespread acceptance of the guiding ideology seems to have been successful, because as Eskilson notes, "Of all the post-war avant-garde art movements, De Stijl had one of the most immediate impacts on typography and graphic design in Europe."[65]

### The Theater for Social Change Movement

Augusto Boal is widely recognised in art history as an innovator and leader of the Theater for Social Change movement. Through the publication of his book *Theatre of the Oppressed* in 1979, Boal introduced actors and actresses to a combined set of beliefs, ideas, values, principles, ethics, morals, and artistic goals that overlapped (i.e., a guiding ideology) and formed the basis for several new approaches (i.e., Image Theater, Invisible Theater, Forum Theater) to facilitate theater that empowers marginalised and oppressed groups.

Boal developed his guiding ideology while serving as the Artistic Director for Arena Theater in São Paulo Brazil from 1956 to 1971. Boal did this with the intention of transferring to the people " ... the means of production in the theatre so that the people themselves may utilize them."[66] In Boal's proposed theater movement, spectators are called to became performers, acting out solutions to social problems, transforming the reality in which they are living. As Gewertz recognizes, "... audience members are free not only to comment on the action, but also to step up on stage and play roles of their choice. In doing so, they discover new ways of resolving the dilemmas that the play presents."[67] In Boal's view, "the theater is a weapon, and it is the people who should wield it."[68]

To facilitate diffusion of his guiding ideology, Boal set up a center for the practice of Image Theater, Invisible Theater, and Forum Theater in Paris, and organised international Theater of the Oppressed festivals in the early to mid-1980s.[69] In addition, Boal taught actors/actresses and non-actor/actresses how to facilitate these new forms of theater in public spaces.[70] Arguably, this is not only evidence of diffusion but also evidence of diffusion via the systematic training of pioneers, many of whom diffused Boal's guiding ideology within their own social networks, speeding up the rate of acceptance worldwide. Sophie Cordray recognises and points to evidence of widespread acceptance of Boal's guiding ideology when recognising, "Over the years, Theatre of the Oppressed has become more professional and more institutionalized."[71] Continuing, Cordray points us to evidence of diffusion and acceptance spanning the globe when recognising, "Theatre of the Oppressed has spread all around the world. Among the most evocative examples of this practice since the 1990s are the Indian one – The Jana Sanskriti, founded by Sanjoy Ganguly – and the Brazilian one – Rio de Janeiro C.T.O. used to work with the Landless Movement (M.S.T.)."[72]

## Notes

1  James DeFronzo and Jungyun Gill, *Social Problems and Social Movements* (London, UK: Rowman & Littlefield, n.d.), 27.
2  DeFronzo and Jungyun Gill, 41–43.
3  Donatella della Porta et al., eds., *The Wiley-Blackwell Encyclopedia of Social and Political Movements* (Hoboken, NJ: Wiley-Blackwell, 2013), 106, 1334.
4  Donatella della Porta et al., 113.
5  Donatella della Porta et al., 1335.
6  Donatella della Porta et al., 1335.
7  Victoria D. Alexander, *Sociology of the Arts: Exploring Fine and Popular Forms* (Malden, MA: Blackwell, 2003), chap. 7.
8  Amy Dempsey, *Styles, Schools & Movements: The Essential Encyclopaedic Guide to Modern Art* (New York, NY: Thames & Hudson Ltd., n.d.).
9  Howard S. Becker, *Art Worlds*, 25th Anniversary (Berkeley, CA: University of California Press, 2008).
10  Amy Dempsey, *Styles, Schools & Movements: The Essential Encyclopaedic Guide to Modern Art.*
11  Julie Caulier-Grice et al., "Defining Social Innovation," White Paper (The Young Foundation, 2012), 23–24, https://youngfoundation.org/wp-content/uploads/2012/12/TEPSIE.D1.1.Report.DefiningSocialInnovation.Part-1-defining-social-innovation.pdf.
12  Amy Dempsey, *Styles, Schools & Movements: The Essential Encyclopaedic Guide to Modern Art.*
13  Joyce S. McKnight and Joanna McKnight Plummer, *Community Organizing: Theory and Practice*, Kindle (New York, NY: Pearson, 2015).
14  Jonathan Paquette and Eleonora Redaelli, *Arts Management and Cultural Policy Research* (NY: Palgrave Macmillian, 2015), chap. 4.
15  Amy Dempsey, *Styles, Schools & Movements: The Essential Encyclopaedic Guide to Modern Art*, 14.
16  Alexander, *Sociology of the Arts: Exploring Fine and Popular Forms*, 113.
17  Alexander, 113.

18 Diana Crane, *The Transformation of the Avant-Garde: The New York Art World, 1940–1985* (Chicago, IL: Unversity of Chicago Press, 1989).
19 Alexander, *Sociology of the Arts: Exploring Fine and Popular Forms*, 113.
20 Becker, *Art Worlds*, 301.
21 Larisa V. Shavinina, *The International Handbook on Innovation* (Kidlington, Oxford: Elsevier Science Ltd, 2003), 31.
22 Donatella della Porta et al., *The Wiley-Blackwell Encyclopedia of Social and Political Movements*, 304.
23 Donatella della Porta et al., 304.
24 Donatella della Porta et al., 389.
25 Donatella della Porta et al., 390.
26 Amy Dempsey, *Styles, Schools & Movements: The Essential Encyclopaedic Guide to Modern Art*.
27 John Butman, *Breaking Out: How to Build Influence in a World of Competing Ideas*, Kindle (Boston, MA: Harvard Business School Publishing, 2013), chap. 1, para 7.
28 Everett M. Rodgers, *Diffusion of Innovations*, 5th Kindle ed. (New York, NY: Free Press, 2003), chaps. 1, section 7.
29 Amy Dempsey, *Styles, Schools & Movements: The Essential Encyclopaedic Guide to Modern Art*; Everett M. Rodgers, *Diffusion of Innovations*.
30 Diana Crane, *The Transformation of the Avant-Garde: The New York Art World, 1940–1985*; Amy Dempsey, *Styles, Schools & Movements: The Essential Encyclopaedic Guide to Modern Art*.
31 It is important to note that manifestos have not always been presented publicly in essay format. For example, in 1984 an anonymous group of American women artists (now widely known as the *Guerrilla Girls*) began publishing a series of manifestos in the form of slogan artworks. For readers interested in additional references, in 2011 author Alex Danchev published a book that includes 100 manifestos of artists. For a more global reference, Jessica Lack's 2017 book *Why Are We Artists?* provides 100 manifestos written by artists from around the world over the last 100 years. Notably, Lack's book challenges two prevalent assertions in Western Art history; (1) that the artist manifesto is a Western phenomenon rather than a global one, and (2) that the artist manifesto is no longer relevant in the 21st-century contemporary art era. Lack challenges both of these assertions when stating, "These manifestos written between 1909–2012 come from all around the world" (p. xiii).
32 Harriet Baker, "10 Game-Changing Art Manifestos," Royal Academy.org, 2015, https://www.royalacademy.org.uk/article/ten-game-changing-manifestos.
33 Everett M. Rodgers, *Diffusion of Innovations*, 177.
34 Everett M. Rodgers, 177.
35 Everett M. Rodgers, 222.
36 Susie Hodge, *The Short Story of Modern Art* (London: Laurence King Publishing, 2019), 7.
37 Christopher Janaway and Sandra Shapshay, "Introduction," in *Aesthetics: A Comprehensive Anthology*, 2nd ed. (Hoboken, NJ: Blackwell Publishing, 2020), 202.
38 Johnathan Fenderson, *Building the Black Arts Movement: Hoyt Fuller and the Cultural Politics of the 1960s* (Urbana, IL: University of Illinois, 2019), 16.

39  Amy Dempsey, *Styles, Schools & Movements: The Essential Encyclopaedic Guide to Modern Art*, 105.
40  Amy Dempsey, 91.
41  Pierre Bourdieu, *Distinction: A Social Critique of the Judgement of Taste* (Cambridge, MA: Harvard University Press, 1984).
42  Amy Dempsey, *Styles, Schools & Movements: The Essential Encyclopaedic Guide to Modern Art*, 77.
43  Amy Dempsey, 101.
44  The Editors of Encyclopaedia Britannica, "Dada," Britannica, August 30, 2019, https://www.britannica.com/art/Dada.
45  The Editors of Encyclopaedia Britannica; Amy Dempsey, *Styles, Schools & Movements: The Essential Encyclopaedic Guide to Modern Art*; Hodge, *The Short Story of Modern Art*.
46  Emily Hage, "The Magazine as Strategy: Tristan Tzara's Dada and the Seminal Role of Dada Art Journals in the Dada Movement," *The Journal of Modern Periodical Studies* 2, no. 1 (2011): 34, https://doi.org/10.5325/jmodeperistud.2.1.0033.
47  Tate Staff, "Dada," Museum Website, Tate, accessed October 8, 2021, https://www.tate.org.uk/art/art-terms/d/dada; Amy Dempsey, *Styles, Schools & Movements: The Essential Encyclopaedic Guide to Modern Art*; Hodge, *The Short Story of Modern Art*.
48  Emily Hage, "The Magazine as Strategy: Tristan Tzara's Dada and the Seminal Role of Dada Art Journals in the Dada Movement," 34.
49  The Editors of Encyclopaedia Britannica, "Dada"; Amy Dempsey, *Styles, Schools & Movements: The Essential Encyclopaedic Guide to Modern Art*.
50  Emily Hage, "The Magazine as Strategy: Tristan Tzara's Dada and the Seminal Role of Dada Art Journals in the Dada Movement," 34.
51  Jeffrey Stewart, *The New Negro: The Life of Alain Locke* (New York: Oxford University Press, 2018).
52  Jeffrey Stewart.
53  Jeffrey Stewart, 522.
54  Jeffrey Stewart, 522.
55  W.E.B. Du Bois, "Criteria for Negro Art," in *Aesthetics: A Comprehensive Anthology*, ed. Steven M. Cahn, Stephanie Ross, and Sandra Shapshay, 2nd ed. (Hoboken, NJ: Wiley-Blackwell, 2020), 427.
56  Jeffrey Stewart, *The New Negro: The Life of Alain Locke*, 526.
57  Jeffrey Stewart, 527.
58  Jeffrey Stewart, 542.
59  Amy Dempsey, *Styles, Schools & Movements: The Essential Encyclopaedic Guide to Modern Art*.
60  Stephen J. Eskilson, *Graphic Design: A New History*, 3rd ed. (New Haven, CT: Yale University Press, 2019).
61  Amy Dempsey, *Styles, Schools & Movements: The Essential Encyclopaedic Guide to Modern Art*, 121.
62  Amy Dempsey, 121.
63  Stephen J. Eskilson, *Graphic Design: A New History*, 171.
64  Stephen J. Eskilson, 171.
65  Stephen J. Eskilson, 171.
66  Augusto Boal, *Theatre of the Oppressed* (New York: Theatre Communications Group, 1979), 122.

67 Ken Gewertz, "Augusto Boal's 'Theatre of the Oppressed,'" *The Harvard Gazette*, December 11, 2003, https://news.harvard.edu/gazette/story/2003/12/augusto-boals-theatre-of-the-oppressed/.
68 Augusto Boal, *Theatre of the Oppressed*, 122.
69 The Editors of Encyclopaedia Britannica, "Augusto Boal," *Encyclopaedia Britannica*, accessed October 9, 2021, https://www.britannica.com/biography/Augusto-Boal.
70 The Editors of Encyclopaedia Britannica; Gewertz, Ken, "Augusto Boal's 'Theatre of the Oppressed.'"
71 Sophie Coudray, "The Theatre of the Oppressed," January 28, 2017, https://www.culturematters.org.uk/index.php/arts/theatre/item/2455-the-theatre-of-the-oppressed.
72 Sophie Coudray.

## References

Alexander, Victoria D. *Sociology of the Arts: Exploring Fine and Popular Forms*. Malden, MA: Blackwell, 2003.

Baker, Harriet. "10 Game-Changing Art Manifestos." *Royal Academy.org*, 2015. https://www.royalacademy.org.uk/article/ten-game-changing-manifestos.

Becker, Howard S. *Art Worlds*. 25th Anniversary. Berkeley, CA: University of California Press, 2008.

Boal, Augusto. *Theatre of the Oppressed*. New York, NY: Theatre Communications Group, 1979.

Bourdieu, Pierre. *Distinction: A Social Critique of the Judgement of Taste*. Cambridge, MA: Harvard University Press, 1984.

Butman, John. *Breaking Out: How to Build Influence in a World of Competing Ideas*. Kindle. Boston, MA: Harvard Business School Publishing, 2013.

Caulier-Grice, Julie, Anna Davies, Robert Patrick, and Will Norman. "Defining Social Innovation." *White Paper. The Young Foundation*, 2012. https://youngfoundation.org/wp-content/uploads/2012/12/TEPSIE.D1.1.Report.DefiningSocialInnovation.Part-1-defining-social-innovation.pdf.

Coudray, Sophie. "The Theatre of the Oppressed," January 28, 2017. https://www.culturematters.org.uk/index.php/arts/theatre/item/2455-the-theatre-of-the-oppressed.

Crane, Diana. *The Transformation of the Avant-Garde: The New York Art World, 1940–1985*. Chicago, IL: University of Chicago Press, 1989.

DeFronzo, James, and Jungyun Gill. *Social Problems and Social Movements*. London, UK: Rowman & Littlefield, n.d.

Dempsey, Amy. *Styles, Schools & Movements: The Essential Encyclopaedic Guide to Modern Art*. New York, NY: Thames & Hudson Ltd., n.d.

Du Bois, W.E.B. "Criteria for Negro Art." In *Aesthetics: A Comprehensive Anthology*, edited by Steven M. Cahn, Stephanie Ross, and Sandra Shapshay, 2nd ed., 423–28. Hoboken, NJ: Wiley-Blackwell, 2020.

Eskilson, Stephen J. *Graphic Design: A New History*. 3rd ed. New Haven, CT: Yale University Press, 2019.

Fenderson, Johnathan. *Building the Black Arts Movement: Hoyt Fuller and the Cultural Politics of the 1960s.* Urbana, IL: University of Illinois, 2019.

Gewertz, Ken. "Augusto Boal's 'Theatre of the Oppressed.'" *The Harvard Gazette*, December 11, 2003. https://news.harvard.edu/gazette/story/2003/12/augusto-boals-theatre-of-the-oppressed/.

Hage, Emily. "The Magazine as Strategy: Tristan Tzara's Dada and the Seminal Role of Dada Art Journals in the Dada Movement." *The Journal of Modern Periodical Studies* 2, no. 1 (2011): 33–53. 10.5325/jmodeperistud. 2.1.0033.

Hodge, Susie. *The Short Story of Modern Art.* London: Laurence King Publishing, 2019.

Janaway, Christopher, and Sandra Shapshay. "Introduction." In *Aesthetics: A Comprehensive Anthology*, 2nd ed., 199–203. Hoboken, NJ: Blackwell Publishing, 2020.

McKnight, Joyce S., and Joanna McKnight Plummer. *Community Organizing: Theory and Practice.* Kindle. New York, NY: Pearson, 2015.

Paquette, Jonathan and Eleonora Redaelli. *Arts Management and Cultural Policy Research.* NY: Palgrave Macmillian, 2015.

Porta, Donatella della, Klandermans Bert, Doug McAdam, and David A. Snow, eds. *The Wiley-Blackwell Encyclopedia of Social and Political Movements.* Hoboken, NJ: Wiley-Blackwell, 2013.

Rodgers, Everett M. *Diffusion of Innovations.* 5th, Kindle ed. New York: Free Press, 2003.

Shavinina, Larisa V. *The International Handbook on Innovation.* Kidlington, Oxford: Elsevier Science Ltd, 2003.

Stewart, Jeffrey. *The New Negro: The Life of Alain Locke.* New York: Oxford University Press, 2018.

Tate Staff. "Dada." *Museum Website.* Tate. Accessed October 8, 2021. https://www.tate.org.uk/art/art-terms/d/dada.

The Editors of Encyclopaedia Britannica. "Augusto Boal." *Encyclopaedia Britannica.* Accessed October 9, 2021. https://www.britannica.com/biography/Augusto-Boal.

The Editors of Encyclopaedia Britannica. "Dada." *Britannica*, August 30, 2019. https://www.britannica.com/art/Dada.

# 5    A Theory of Audience Experience Innovation

## Theory

Arguably, one way to achieve innovation in the arts is to pursue audience experience innovation. In theory, **audience experience innovation** is *the development, diffusion, and widespread integration of a structured experience design for visual, literary, or performing arts audiences.* This type of innovation occurs when the innovator(s) identifies a conventional experience design for arts audiences, experiments with and adds new defining elements to the experience, tests that design on a group of audience members, captures social proof of esthetic experience, and then diffuses the new experience design and social proof in networks populated by arts administrators. As more and more arts administrators become aware of both the new experience design and associated social proof, some will become early adopters by integrating the new experience design and by using it as a guide for arts presenting.

## Theoretical framework

Although there are many different types of arts organisations, presenting arts organisations tend to structure and present experiences to diverse arts audiences. From the perspective of arts administrators (also sometimes called arts managers) who work within presenting arts organisations, **arts presenting** generally refers to *the process of planning and presenting visual, literary, or performing arts experiences to an individual or group.* Such presentations are the primary means by which presenting arts organisations either satisfy known audience demand and/or carry out their organisation's not-for-profit mission.

DOI: 10.4324/9781003142393-5

## The type of experiences arts audiences desire

Research suggests that when audiences attend exhibitions, events, or performances presented by arts organisations, they expect to have a *special kind of sensory experience* historically referred to by philosophers of art as **esthetic** in nature.[1] While originally associated with Eurocentric notions of beauty and taste, contemporary scholars in the field of esthetics have since broadened their view of the concept of *esthetics*. As Bence Nanay references, "Aesthetics is about some special kinds of experiences. Ones we care about a lot. The Greek 'aesthesis' means 'perception' and when German philosopher Alexander Baumgarten (1714-62) introduced the concept of 'aesthetics' in 1750, what he meant by it was precisely the study of sensory experience (scientia cognitionis sensitivae)."[2] Although there are many proposed concepts of esthetic experience, Alan Goldman prefers to use a concept derived from the beliefs of John Dewey and Monroe Beardsley. In Goldman's view, "... such experience involves the active and simultaneous engagement of all of our mental faculties: perception, imagination, emotion and cognition. Such full engagement with a work of art, which may seem an alternative world to the viewer, is the mark of aesthetic experience."[3]

## Considering the relationship between the perception of art and esthetic experience

While *esthetics* and *the philosophy of art* are not the same concept, esthetics is often associated with art in art history because *the perception of art has been known to trigger special kinds of sensory experiences*. For example, in the book *Art as Experience*, John Dewey argues that the experience of perceiving art (i.e., an act of consumption) is an esthetic experience in and of itself.[4] Observations by Kenneth Foster suggest that artistic performance has the potential to trigger esthetic experience, or perhaps, to trigger simultaneous engagement of all of the viewer's mental faculties: perception, imagination, emotion, and cognition. For example, when discussing why performance matters, Foster notes:

> When we speak of the unique joy of live performance, this is what we actually mean: being in a space with others and having a uniquely shared live artistic experience together. The performance creates this temporary, fragile community of the moment; a deeply profound moment that subsequently dissolves and disperses with only the imperfect memory of that moment to sustain us.[5]

The performance experience can also deeply affect us emotionally, often touching on feelings we have stored deep in our psyches. Performances help us tap into those feelings; being engaged in this alternate reality grants us permission to act and react in ways we might not ordinarily. Open demonstrations of tears or laughter, joyous celebration, pain and sorrow too deep and profound to be actually expressed or shared even with our closet confident – all these can and do find their place in how we respond to the performance experience.[6]

In addition to research findings in the arts leadership, performance studies, and esthetics literature,[7] support for the ability of artworks to trigger esthetic experience can also be found in the psychology of the arts literature.[8] For example, in the book *How Art Works*, Ellen Winner found that artworks create an imaginative experience for both the maker and the perceiver.[9] Recall that Goldman believes that the engagement of our imagination is one of the markers of esthetic experience. Winner also observes, "Artworks are experienced in a pretend world. We know that fictional characters are not real, yet they make us frightened, sad, relieved, and happy. We listen to music and experience emotions even though no events are causing us to feel sorrow, joy, or excitement. The imaginative experience caused by art is decoupled from any practical concern – in Immanuel Kant's eighteenth-century words, art is for disinterested contemplation."[10]

While not all art is decoupled from practical concern (e.g., theater for social change, arts-in-health projects), Eurocentric notions of art (e.g., art is for disinterested contemplation) remind us that cultural values influence interpretations of both art and esthetic experience. For example, in the book *Indian Aesthetics and the Philosophy of Art*, editor Arindam Chakrabarti opens the book by stating, "Not so much beautiful or lovely, as amazing and awesome."[11] To be clear, what Chakrabarti is suggesting here, is that based on his observations, encounters with artworks in India can trigger esthetic experiences, and arts audiences in India who have those experiences tend to refer to them - not so much as beautiful or lovely (in the tradition of European esthetics), but rather as amazing and awesome (in the tradition of Indian esthetics). What Chakrabarti is also suggesting in the first chapter of his book, is that if you learn about the cultural and community values of those who live in India, you will be more likely to have an esthetic experience when viewing artworks in India.[12] This is because knowledge of diverse cultural and community values can help us make sense of diverse artworks and trigger diverse esthetic experiences.[13] Notably, when reporting on the various esthetic experiences that can be triggered when perceiving artworks, Winner notes, "People have reported extremely powerful emotional responses while standing in front of paintings – shaking, dizziness and tears."[14] Continuing, Winner asserts, "… the visual arts (like all arts) can move us strongly, and there is fascinating evidence about the areas of the brain that are activated when paintings move us."[15]

## Designing and structuring arts experiences that trigger esthetic experience

In considering how an innovator might design and structure a visual, literary, or performing arts experience that causes audiences to have an esthetic experience, John Dewey provides helpful insight when observing that, "There are common patterns in various experiences, no matter how unlike they are to one another in the details of their subject matter. There are conditions to be met without which an experience cannot come to be."[16] Continuing, Dewey recognises that "An experience has pattern and structure, because it is not just doing and undergoing in alternation, but consists of them in relationship. To put one's hand in the fire that consumes it is not necessarily to have an experience. The action and its consequence must be joined in perception. This relationship is what gives them meaning."[17]

Steve Dixon supports Dewey's position when reflecting on a full-length live digital dance project entitled BIPED that was first presented to an audience in 1998. Dixon recognises the patterns, structures, and relationships that contributed to both the performance experience and the triggering of esthetic experience when recognising, "The powerful aesthetics and poetic interrelationships between Cunningham's dancers and their digital counterparts in BIPED promoted some critics to describe the experience in metaphysical and religious terms."[18] Notably, this live theater experience was designed in collaboration by Merce Cunningham and a company called Riverbed, whose mission was, "to design and develop new media projects primarily for the visual and performing arts."[19] As Dixon notes:

> For Cunningham's dance, named after the software, Riverbed used motion capture techniques to map in three dimensions the movements of three dancers performing some twenty Cunningham movement sequences in a studio.[20]

These were projected during the BIPED live dance performance, the projections being cast onto a front scrim, allowing the live dancers to appear to interrelate with the virtual dancers in various abstractions and spatial configurations.[21]

The projections lasted for approximately half of the duration of the live performance, and Cunningham only determined their sequential order just before the first performance, selection being made on a chance basis.[22]

It is important to note that experiences do not have to be designed or structured in order to trigger esthetic experience. Sometimes, esthetic experience is triggered spontaneously or through our everyday activities. In the article *Everyday Aesthetics*, Yuriko Saito reminds us that "the aesthetic and the practical cannot be neatly separated," such as the esthetic experience of opening a Japanese package.[23] However, arguably, visual, literary, and performing arts experiences can be both designed and structured to trigger esthetic experience for audiences, either at one point in time or over a longer period of time on a re-occurring basis. J. Rossman and Mathew Duerden help us to consider how these experiences might be designed by proposing six core elements necessary to design an experience: "people, place, objects, rules, relationships and blocking."[24] Rossman and Duerden define these six core elements as:[25]

- *People*, which refers to all individuals involved in the experience, including participants and stagers, whether physically present.
- *Place*, which refers to the place in physical space and chronological time in which the experience occurs.
- *Objects*, which refer to physical, social, and symbolic objects that play a recognised role in the experience.
- *Rules*, which refer to the rules that influence experiences, from codified laws to social expectations.
- *Relationships*, which refer to the relationships people in the experience share that influence their interactions.
- *Blocking*, *which* refers to the choreography of people's location and movement through an experience.

While there may be additional elements necessary for designing different types of experiences, Rossman and Duerden believe that each of the core elements listed above is unique and important, "... so important that if one is altered, the experience fundamentally changes."[26] Foster offers support for Rossman and Duerden's position when reflecting on the contributing elements that caused him to have an esthetic experience while watching a contemporary African dance performance presented by the dance company *Compagnie TchéTché.*[27] Foster notes:

> [Place] I joined a small audience of people in what was clearly one of the least desirable spaces of the festival venue. Sitting in the bleachers in something of a crude "black box" environment, we watched as the performers made last-minute preparations. The lights dimmed, musicians appeared and the performance began.[28]

> [Blocking] What happened in the next 40 minutes I can only describe as transcendent. Even today, many years later, I still count this experience as one of the most meaningful arts experiences of my lifetime. Accompanied by live music both plaintive and powerful, four extraordinary women entered the space. Their physical appearances, while varied, conveyed an unmistakable sense of internal strength. For the next 40 minutes or so, they took us on an unforgettable journey into their lives, their hearts, their souls and the soul of their country, Côte d'Ivoire.[29]

> Moving purposefully through the space, they performed a dance that seemed to possess both anguish and love. Their bodies made contact, separated and then came together again and again, embracing, slapping, falling and catching each other, reaching, it seemed to me, for depth of connection and love that even physical movement did not seem capable of expressing.[30]

> [Relationships] As I noted previously, in relation to Compagnie TchéTché, and their performance of Dimi, it seemed as if we, as a single entity, were trying to reach the artists and they were trying to reach us. In essence, we were building together a community of the moment and we as the audience are deeply affected by the artists' ability, or not, to engage us a "community of the moment."[31]

> [Objects] I reflected too on what really happened in the performance itself. What elements came together to create this unspoken but deeply felt connection between myself and the performers?[32]

In the book *Arts Management*, Ellen Rosewall reminds us of all the [People] it takes to design and structure an engaging performing arts experience like the one that Foster discusses. As Rosewall rightly notes, "Just like any business, arts organisations require human resources."[33] Howard Becker's observations of cooperative action in art worlds also help us to recognise that these types of experiences rarely happen without cooperation between performing artists, arts administrators, and arts audiences. Moreover, Pierre Bourdieu's observations of rules of order in artistic fields provide empirical support for the [Rules] that guide the structuring of these types of experiences.[34] Kirsty Sedgman supports Bourdieu's position by referencing and discussing the endorsed rules of theater etiquette which guide how Western audiences both respond and are expected to respond while attending the theater.[35]

## Developing a new audience experience design

From the perspective of presenting arts organisations, visual, literary, and performing arts experiences are co-created through intentional design and structured configurations of specific production and marketing elements, such as the selection of one or more genres of art to be presented, planned activities for the artists, a selected performance space or venue, a selected audience seating or standing arrangement, the selection of a particular event day and time, selected marketing features which augment the audiences' pre-presentation and post-presentation experience, and the planned social activities which take place, before, during and/or after the event. Upon recommendations from arts administrators in power, performing arts organisations (re)use certain audience experience designs in order to make arts presenting easier to facilitate, less costly, and more efficient. Over time, the over-use of a particular audience experience design becomes increasingly recognised by art world members as a conventional audience experience in that art world. Joanne Bernstein supports this point when recognising, "Arts organizations have traditionally followed a ritualistic pattern of performance presentation. The symphony concert, in particular, is generally characterised by a short opening work, a concerto with soloist, an intermission, and then a longer symphonic piece, all performed by up to one hundred musicians identically dressed in formal attire."[36] As Bernstein rightly suggests, "There are many ways this ritual can be altered to enliven the experience."[37]

Recognising an innovation opportunity, the innovator begins to identify the people, place, objects, rules, relationships, and blocking that contribute to a conventional audience experience in an art world. Equipped with the knowledge of contributing production and marketing elements, the innovator begins to play with the audience experience design through iterative rounds of creative experimentation. In doing so, the innovator takes an effectual approach, arranging the contributing elements in unconventional ways, testing and (re)adjusting the audience experience design according to what they learn, until finally recognising a new way to experience the presentation of one or more art forms in a way in which target audiences perceive as more interesting, engaging, relevant and accessible.

Next, the innovator will work to capture social proof that the new audience experience design triggers esthetic experience for target audiences. Alan Goldman suggests that this social proof can be documented in three ways: (1) by capturing objective accounts which emphasise the content of the experience (e.g., the specific resources and materials needed to create the experience), (2) by capturing subjective accounts which emphasise the phenomenological nature of the experience (e.g., what audiences feel before, during and after the experience), and (3) by capturing external attitude accounts which emphasise the value of the experience (e.g., how good or bad audiences believe the experience was).[38] Notably, Goldman posits that the subjective account is the most productive way to document esthetic experience because it draws our attention to "... the active and simultaneous engagement of all of our mental faculties: perception, imagination, emotion and cognition," and because it can help us differentiate the esthetic experience from non-esthetic experience.[39]

### Diffusing the new audience experience design

Next, the innovator diffuses both the new audience experience design and associated social proof in networks populated by arts administrators. Given that arts administrators tend to make production management and marketing decisions for presenting arts organisations, arts administrators seem to be an appropriate target group for the diffusion of new audience experience designs. However, in order to convince arts administrators to replace an existing design or add a new design, the innovator will likely need to present social proof that the new audience experience design triggers esthetic experience for one or more audience groups. As Bonita Kolb notes, social proof may often take the form of stories, which "... contain information on product usage ...," and "... become emotionally compelling and promote purchase in ways that facts and figures alone cannot do."[40] In addition to stories, Kolb reminds us that social proof can also take the form of expert or celebrity endorsements, "... which have a psychological basis for their success in motivating purchase."[41] Motivated by social proof, some arts administrators will become early adopters by being amongst the first to integrate the new audience experience design and use it as a guide for arts presenting.

## Navigating resistance to integration

Research findings by Everett Rodgers suggest that in general, the diffusion of innovations is full of uncertainty, so it's likely that some arts administrators will resist integration while others will become early integrators.[42] Research suggests that arts administrators working within not-for-profit arts organisations may actually be more likely to resist integration than arts administrators working within for-profit arts organisations. For example, in their research on innovation in non-profit and for-profit organisations, Clyde Hull & Brian Lio found that "Non-profits have less freedom in market consideration, as their market is usually an intrinsic part of the organization's mission, laid out in the charter."[43] Thus, if the social proof does not include stories or endorsements from specific groups of people targeted by a not-for-profit arts organisation's mission, arts administrators who work within that organisation may consider the new audience experience design to be irrelevant, and may resist integration. In addition, Hull and Lio remind us that in comparison to for-profit organisations, "Non-profits are typically risk-adverse and constrained by an extensive net of responsibility that holds them extremely accountable for any failure."[44] Thus, if the arts administrator who works in a not-for-profit presenting arts organisation believes integration of the new audience experience design is too risky, too resource intensive, or too disruptive to normal day-to-day operations, the arts administrator may resist integration.

## The integration process for a presenting arts organisation

Once arts administrators are convinced by social proof that a new audience experience design triggers esthetic experience for one or more targeted audience group(s), they will recommend that their presenting arts organisation integrate it into their program plans. In discussing arts programming, Steven Morrison points out that "... performing arts administrators appreciate systematic processes" because those processes can often lead to desired outcomes.[45] However, based on Rodgers' research findings, this integration process will likely be different for formal presenting arts organisations (e.g., those with defined goals, roles, responsibilities, and rules of order) than for informal presenting arts organisations (e.g., those with little to no defined goals, roles, responsibilities, and rules of order).[46] To help us consider plausible differences, Rodgers offers a theoretical framework for how formal organisations adopt innovations and proposes a sequential process consisting of five stages:[47]

- **The agenda-setting stage**, in which the organisation identifies its own problems and needs, and then searches the environment for an innovation to address those problems or needs
- **The matching stage**, in which the organisation identifies an innovation that it believes will address its problems or needs
- **The redefining/restructuring stage,** in which either the innovation is modified in order to be integrated into the existing structure of the organisation, or the organisation is re-structured in order to integrate the innovation
- **The clarifying stage,** when the relationship between the innovation and the organisation is defined more clearly
- **The routinising stage,** when the innovation is fully incorporated into the regular activities of the organisation and loses its independent identity

Given Rodgers' insight, it might take a longer time to integrate a new audience experience design into a formal presenting arts organisation than it would for an informal presenting arts organisation. For formal presenting arts organisations, integration might look more like a new program model or program format. In support, Gaylene Carpenter points out that "... program format involves choosing among the various available program patterns," and "... patterns set the tone for the experience."[48] In cases where this is true, the innovator's original experience design may be modified to some degree during the redefining/restructuring stage that Rodgers discusses. In theory, if the new audience experience design makes it to the routinising stage referenced by Rodgers, it means that the innovator was successful in facilitating audience experience innovation in a formal presenting arts organisation. However, if innovations lose their independent identity in the routinising stage, the innovator's experience design may look radically different than the one initially diffused.

## Conclusion: So what does success look like?

Given research findings on the diffusion of innovations, it's likely that the process of audience experience innovation ends after most presenting arts organisations in an art world begin to utilise the new experience design on a re-occurring basis. In cases where this milestone occurs, I would call it a success because it means that the innovator has changed the way these organisations present the arts to audiences. This type of innovation can have a significant impact on existing arts audiences because it can provide them with new types of esthetic experiences either desired or previously unrealised. This type of innovation can also disrupt the normal way of arts presenting in an art world and change arts audiences' expectations. In theory, as awareness of the social proof increases in art worlds, the rate of integration will increase amongst presenting arts organisations in that art world.

## Case studies of audience experience innovation

### The Bayreuth Festpielhaus experience design

Digital performance historians like Steve Dixon consider Richard Wagner's 19th-century theater design to be an innovation in experience design.[49] Recognised by theater historians as the seminal influence on experimental theater, Wagner's guiding concept (expressed in such writings as *The Artwork of the Future*) advocated for the creative unification of multiple art forms and the implementation of a wholly immersive audience experience (i.e., user immersion) through a variety of technological and artistic strategies. To gain social proof of esthetic experience, Wagner built his own theater in 1876 (called *Bayreuth Festpielhaus*) and began to test his unique experience design on German theater audiences.

According to Dixon, "The space was designed with a fan-shaped auditorium to ensure perfect sightlines from every seat."[50] This innovative design eliminated visual distractions common to most 19th-century theaters in the West (e.g., pillars, balconies, boxes). In addition, Dixon notes that "Unlike conventional theater orchestra pits, the music is directed first onto the stage itself in order to merge with the singers' voices, before the composite sound resonates back out into the auditorium."[51] Perhaps this is why Dixon calls Wagner,

"... the first theater producer to design and construct a sophisticated audio mixing system."[52] Continuing, Dixon notes, "The acoustically sophisticated theatre also utilized the latest innovations in stage machinery to intensify the illusion of Wagner's mythic images."[53]

Based on a review of Dixon's book *Digital Performance*, the history of digital performance includes innovators (like Wagner) who recognised the limitations of conventional audience experience designs, learned about new technologies, experimented with them, and then integrated them into new audience experience designs.[54] These innovators did not integrate new technologies simply because they could (i.e., tech for tech's sake). Rather, they did so in order to *enhance and improve the esthetic experience for audiences.* Technology was a means to an end. As Steve Dixon states, "Digital performance is an extension of a continuing history of the adoption and adaptation of technologies to increase performance and visual art's esthetic effect and sense of spectacle, its emotional and sensorial impact, its play of meanings and symbolic associations, and its intellectual power."[55]

### The Drive-in-Movie Theater experience design

In 1933, Richard Hollingshead opened the first drive-in movie theater in Camden, New Jersey. Robin Read notes that on opening day, customers paid "... 25 cents per car as well as per person to see British comedy *Wives Beware* under the stars."[56] According to Jim Kopp of the *United Drive-in Theatre Owners Association*, Hollingshead's mother could not fit into the conventional indoor theater seats, so Hollingshead "... stuck her in a car and put a 1928 projector on the hood of a car, and tied two sheets to trees in his yard."[57] After experimenting with this experience design for a few years, Hollingshead "... created a ramp system for cars to park at different heights so everyone could see the screen."[58]

According to Read, Hollingshead, "... patented his concept in May 1933 and opened the gates to his theater the next month."[59] The second drive-in *Shankweiler's* started a year later, but the drive-in movie theater experience design didn't really catch on until the widespread adoption of car speakers in the 1940s. After this technology adoption, the new experience design caught on with a wide range of movie audiences, in part because the esthetic experience it triggered was attractive to young couples and families with small children, who could avoid the need for a babysitter.[60] Motivated by social proof of esthetic experience, many entertainment entrepreneurs integrated Hollingshead's experience design into their drive-in theaters in the

1950s. According to Ronald Bergan's research in Film history, "Some 4,000 drive-ins were constructed across America, but their popularity started to decline in the 1960s. Only a few still exist today, frequented by nostalgic audiences."[61]

### The Sleep No More experience design

According to Jonathan Mandell, immersive theater "... stimulates all five senses – sight and sound as with conventional theater pieces, but also touch, and frequently taste and even smell."[62] Led by Artistic Director Felix Barrett since the year 2000, punchdrunk is a theater company that has become widely recognised around the world for pioneering an innovative form of immersive theater "... in which roaming audiences experience epic storytelling inside sensory theatrical worlds."[63] According to punchdrunk's website, the company is "... widely recognized as the explosive spark which ignited the immersive entertainment industry by disrupting the theatrical norm."[64] The company is best known for its production of *Sleep No More*, a live theatrical version of Macbeth told within a 1930s setting with a film noir esthetic. Numerous critics speak to the unique esthetic experience. For example, Scott Brown writes:

> What in Hecate's name is *Sleep No More*? A dance-theater horror show? A wordless, nonlinear mash-up of *Macbeth* and the darker psychosexual corners of Hitchcock? A six-story Jazz Age haunted house for grown-ups and anyone who's ever entertained sick cineast-y fantasies of living inside a Kubrick movie? Tis all these, and more besides: a deed without a name, to quote an infernal authority. (Also: 'tis sold-out, but set to extend, so get your trigger finger ready.) The UK's Punchdrunk theater collective — famed for these sorts of immersive, site-specific experiments back on their native sod — has finally brought *Sleep* to the city that never does, and now, most certainly, won't: The show infects your dreams.[65]

Notably, the first production of *Sleep No More* took place in London in 2003, with a second rendition presented in Boston in 2009. Since then, the production has been set up in Shanghai, China, and is (according to punchdrunk) currently the longest-running international show in Shanghai's history.[66] Ruthie Fierberg of PlayBill provides insight on the innovative audience experience design:

Punchdrunk staged *Sleep No More* throughout the McKittrick Hotel. There is no stage; you don't take your seats. Every room in the multi-floor "playspace" is the "set," and decorated to create the world of *Macbeth* in the hotel. Whether exploring the space on your own, or chasing actors to witness the action, audiences climb a lot of stairs and may even jog to follow performers.[67]

The audience is an integral piece of this theatre. Actors will approach individual attendees, whisper in your ear, kiss you on the hand. While performers gauge the comfort of those they get close to, if you don't want this type of interaction—no problem. Situate yourself within the crowd instead of at the very front.[68]

Because the action moves all around the hotel, *Sleep No More* is crafted as choose-your-own-adventure. While you can attend with friends, on a date, or in a group, don't expect to stay together—and don't be that person that holds hands with your partner the entire show. A physical link will block other people from navigating the space, since performers move quickly from room to room. Embrace the individuality of your path and go where the action or your interests take you; there's no talking inside and you'll have more to discuss after the show if you see different things![69]

## Notes

1 John Dewey, *Art as Experience*, Kindle (New York, NY: Penguin Books, 2005); Alan H. Goldman, "What Is Aesthetic Experience?," in *Aesthetics: A Comprehensive Anthology* (Hoboken, NJ: Wiley-Blackwell, 2020), 581–88.
2 Bence Nanay, *Aesthetics: A Very Short Introduction*, Kindle (Oxford, UK: Oxford University Press, 2019), 2.
3 Alan H. Goldman, "What Is Aesthetic Experience?," 582.
4 Dewey, *Art as Experience*.
5 Kenneth Foster, *Arts Leadership: Creating Sustainable Arts Organizations* (New York, NY: Routledge, 2018), 50.
6 Kenneth Foster, 48.
7 Tobin Siebers, *Disability Aesthetics* (Michigan: The University of Michigan, 2010); Paul Taylor, *Black Is Beautiful: A Philosophy of Black Aesthetics* (Hoboken, NJ: John Wiley & Sons, 2016); Arindam Chakrabarti, ed., *The Bloomsbury Research Handbook of Indian Aesthetics and the Philosophy of Art* (Bloomsbury Academic, 2018).
8 Hans Kreitler and Shulamith Kreitler, *Psychology of the Arts* (Durham, NC: Duke University Press, 1972).
9 Ellen Winner, *How Art Works* (New York, NY: Oxford University Press, 2019), 12.
10 Winner, 12.

11 Arindam Chakrabarti, *The Bloomsbury Research Handbook of Indian Aesthetics and the Philosophy of Art*, 1.

12 Arindam Chakrabarti, *The Bloomsbury Research Handbook of Indian Aesthetics and the Philosophy of Art*.

13 Taylor, *Black Is Beautiful: A Philosophy of Black Aesthetics*; Chakrabarti, Arindam, *The Bloomsbury Research Handbook of Indian Aesthetics and the Philosophy of Art*; Siebers, *Disability Aesthetics*; Alanna Cant, *The Value of Aesthetics* (Austin, TX: University of Texas Press, 2019).

14 Winner, *How Art Works*, 77.

15 Winner, 77.

16 Dewey, *Art as Experience*, 45.

17 Dewey, 46.

18 Steve Dixon, *Digital Performance: A History of New Media in Theater, Dance, Performance Art, and Installation* (Cambridge, MA: The MIT Press, 2015), 191.

19 Steve Dixon, 187.

20 Steve Dixon, 188.

21 Steve Dixon, 190.

22 Steve Dixon, 190.

23 Yuriko Saito, "Everyday Aesthetics," in *Aesthetics: A Comprehensive Anthology* (Hoboken, NJ: Wiley-Blackwell, 2020), 780.

24 Robert J. Rossman and Mathew D. Duerden, *Designing Experiences*, Kindle (New York Chichester, West Sussex: Columbia University Press, 2019), 59.

25 Robert J. Rossman and Mathew D. Duerden, 60.

26 Robert J. Rossman and Mathew D. Duerden, 59.

27 Kenneth Foster, *Arts Leadership: Creating Sustainable Arts Organizations*.

28 Kenneth Foster, 46.

29 Kenneth Foster, 46.

30 Kenneth Foster, 46.

31 Kenneth Foster, 49.

32 Kenneth Foster, 47.

33 Ellen Rosewall, *Arts Management: Uniting Arts and Audiences in the 21st Century* (New York: Oxford University Press, 2014), 86.

34 Pierre Bourdieu, *The Rules of Art: Genesis and Structure of the Literary Field* (Stanford, CA: Stanford University Press, 1996).

35 Kirsty Sedgman, *The Reasonable Audience: Theatre Etiquette, Behaviour Policing and the Live Performance Experience* (Cham, Switzerland: Palgrave Macmillian, 2018).

36 Joanne S. Bernstein, *Standing Room Only*, 2nd ed. (Boston, MA: Palgrave Macmillian, 2014), 178.

37 Joanne S. Bernstein, 178.

38 Alan H. Goldman, "What Is Aesthetic Experience?"

39 Alan H. Goldman, 582–84.

40 Bonita Kolb, *Marketing Strategy for the Creative and Cultural Industries* (New York: Routledge, 2016), 30.

41 Bonita Kolb, 30.

42 Everett M. Rodgers, *Diffusion of Innovations*, 5th, Kindle ed. (New York: Free Press, 2003), 6.

43 Clyde E. Hull and Brian H. Lio, "Innovation in Non-Profit and For-Profit

Organizations: Visionary, Strategic, and Financial Considerations," *Journal of Change Management* 6, no. 1 (2006): 57.
44 Clyde E. Hull and Brian H. Lio, 62.
45 Steven Morrison, "Performing Arts Programming," in *Arts and Cultural Programming: A Leisure Perspective* (Champaign, IL: Human Kinetics, 2008), 201.
46 Udo Staber, *Understanding Organizations: Theories and Images*, Kindle (Thousand Oaks, CA: Sage Publications, 2013); Fariborz Damanpour and Marguerite Schneider, "Characteristics of Innovation and Innovation Adoption in Public Organizations: Assessing the Role of Manager," *Journal of Public Administration Research and Theory* 19, no. 3 (2009): 495–522, https://doi.org/10.1093/jopart/mun021.
47 Everett M. Rodgers, *Diffusion of Innovations*, 421.
48 Gaylene Carpenter, "Programming Tasks and Functions," in *Arts and Cultural Programming: A Leisure Perspective* (Champaign, IL: Human Kinetics, 2008), 43.
49 Steve Dixon, *Digital Performance: A History of New Media in Theater, Dance, Performance Art, and Installation*, 41–45.
50 Steve Dixon, 42.
51 Steve Dixon, 42.
52 Steve Dixon, 42.
53 Steve Dixon, 42.
54 Steve Dixon, *Digital Performance: A History of New Media in Theater, Dance, Performance Art, and Installation*.
55 Steve Dixon, 40.
56 Robin Read, "The History of the Drive-In Movie Theater," *Smithsonian Magazine*, 2008, https://www.smithsonianmag.com/arts-culture/the-history-of-the-drive-in-movie-theater-51331221/.
57 Robin Read.
58 Robin Read.
59 Robin Read.
60 Ronald Bergan, *The Film Book* (New York: Penguin Random House, 2021), 33.
61 Ronald Bergan, 33.
62 Johnathan Mandell, "What Is Immersive Theater? The Six Elements That Define it at Its Best," *New York Theater*, accessed December 10, 2021, https://newyorktheater.me/2019/10/04/what-is-immersive-theater-the-six-elements-that-define-it-at-its-best/.
63 punchdrunk, "Punchdrunk," punchdrunk, accessed December 10, 2021, https://www.punchdrunk.com/about-us/.
64 punchdrunk.
65 Scott Brown, "Theater Review: The Freakily Immersive Experience of Sleep No More," *Vulture*, April 15, 2021, https://www.vulture.com/2011/04/theater_review_the_freakily_im.html.
66 punchdrunk, "Punchdrunk."
67 Ruthie Fierberg, "9 Tips for Attending the Award-Winning Sleep No More," *Playbill*, July 1, 2019, https://www.playbill.com/article/9-tips-for-attending-the-award-winning-sleep-no-more.
68 Ruthie Fierberg.
69 Ruthie Fierberg.

# References

Bergan, Ronald. *The Film Book*. New York: Penguin Random House, 2021.

Bernstein, Joanne S. *Standing Room Only*. 2nd ed. Boston, MA: Palgrave Macmillian, 2014.

Bourdieu, Pierre. *The Rules of Art: Genesis and Structure of the Literary Field*. Stanford, CA: Stanford University Press, 1996.

Brown, Scott. "Theater Review: The Freakily Immersive Experience of Sleep No More." *Vulture*, April 15, 2021. https://www.vulture.com/2011/04/theater_review_the_freakily_im.html

Cant, Alanna. *The Value of Aesthetics*. Austin, TX: University of Texas Press, 2019.

Carpenter, Gaylene. "Programming Tasks and Functions." In *Arts and Cultural Programming: A Leisure Perspective*, 37–50. Champaign, IL: Human Kinetics, 2008.

Chakrabarti, Arindam, ed. *The Bloomsbury Research Handbook of Indian Aesthetics and the Philosophy of Art*. Bloomsbury Academic, 2018.

Damanpour, Fariborz, and Marguerite Schneider. "Characteristics of Innovation and Innovation Adoption in Public Organizations: Assessing the Role of Manager." *Journal of Public Administration Research and Theory* 19, no. 3 (2009): 495–522. 10.1093/jopart/mun021

Dewey, John. *Art as Experience*. Kindle. New York, NY: Penguin Books, 2005.

Dixon, Steve. *Digital Performance: A History of New Media in Theater, Dance, Performance Art, and Installation*. Cambridge, MA: The MIT Press, 2015.

Fierberg, Ruthie. "9 Tips for Attending the Award-Winning Sleep No More." *Playbill*, July 1, 2019. https://www.playbill.com/article/9-tips-for-attending-the-award-winning-sleep-no-more

Foster, Kenneth. *Arts Leadership: Creating Sustainable Arts Organizations*. New York: Routledge, 2018.

Goldman, Alan H. "What Is Aesthetic Experience?" In *Aesthetics: A Comprehensive Anthology*, 581–88. Hoboken, NJ: Wiley-Blackwell, 2020.

Hull, Clyde E., and Brian H. Lio "Innovation in Non-Profit and For-Profit Organizations: Visionary, Strategic, and Financial Considerations." *Journal of Change Management* 6, no. 1 (2006): 53–65.

Kolb, Bonita. *Marketing Strategy for the Creative and Cultural Industries*. New York: Routledge, 2016.

Kreitler, Hans, and Shulamith Kreitler. *Psychology of the Arts*. Durham, NC: Duke University Press, 1972.

Mandell, Johnathan. "What Is Immersive Theater? The Six Elements That Define It at Its Best." *New York Theater*. Accessed December 10, 2021. https://newyorktheater.me/2019/10/04/what-is-immersive-theater-the-six-elements-that-define-it-at-its-best/

Morrison, Steven. "Performing Arts Programming." In *Arts and Cultural Programming: A Leisure Perspective*, 199–216. Champaign, IL: Human Kinetics, 2008.

Nanay, Bence. *Aesthetics: A Very Short Introduction.* Kindle. Oxford, UK: Oxford University Press, 2019.

punchdrunk. "Punchdrunk." *punchdrunk.* Accessed December 10, 2021. https://www.punchdrunk.com/about-us/.

Read, Robin. "The History of the Drive-In Movie Theater." *Smithsonian Magazine*, 2008. https://www.smithsonianmag.com/arts-culture/the-history-of-the-drive-in-movie-theater-51331221/.

Rodgers, Everett M. *Diffusion of Innovations.* 5th, Kindle ed. New York, NY: Free Press, 2003.

Rosewall, Ellen. *Arts Management: Uniting Arts and Audiences in the 21st Century.* New York, NY: Oxford University Press, 2014.

Rossman, Robert J., and Mathew D. Duerden *Designing Experiences.* Kindle. New York Chichester, West Sussex: Columbia University Press, 2019.

Saito, Yuriko. "Everyday Aesthetics." In *Aesthetics: A Comprehensive Anthology*, 777–82. Hoboken, NJ: Wiley-Blackwell, 2020.

Sedgman, Kirsty. *The Reasonable Audience: Theatre Etiquette, Behaviour Policing and the Live Performance Experience.* Cham, Switzerland: Palgrave Macmillian, 2018.

Siebers, Tobin. *Disability Aesthetics.* Michigan: The University of Michigan, 2010.

Staber, Udo. *Understanding Organizations: Theories and Images.* Kindle. Thousand Oaks, CA: Sage Publications, 2013.

Taylor, Paul. *Black Is Beautiful: A Philosophy of Black Aesthetics.* Hoboken, NJ: John Wiley & Sons, 2016.

Winner, Ellen. *How Art Works.* New York: Oxford University Press, 2019.

# 6 Conclusions and Suggested Directions

For far too long innovation efforts in the arts have been misunderstood, overlooked, and marginalised in most of the innovation and entrepreneurship literature. While some innovation scholars have referenced the concept, none to my knowledge have taken on the challenge of writing and publishing formal theories evidenced by case studies in art history. If these formal theories are indeed the first of their kind, I surely hope that they will not be the last ones written, published, and made widely available to people all around the world. Given the impact of the COVID-19 pandemic on art worlds and related industries around the world, the changing demographics in global arts attendance, the new cultural preferences of younger arts audiences, and the economic challenges that most not-for-profit arts organisations are facing today, we need innovation in the arts more than ever. The theories presented in this book help to explain and demystify innovation processes that have occurred in art history. The selected citations used to support the theories provide empirical support for my assertions and conclusions. Based on these theories, I'd like to make some suggestions for innovation researchers and entrepreneurship educators.

## Implications for innovation research

The theory of art innovation should matter to innovation researchers because new art forms are process innovations, and there are so many of these innovations emerging from within communities, regions, states, cities, and countries all around the world. Artists, arts administrators, and cultural policymakers need to know about these new innovations because they often function as a catalyst for the development of new communities of artistic practice. They can stimulate declining creative industries and stagnant cultural economies. They

DOI: 10.4324/9781003142393-6

can also provide entrepreneurs with opportunities to create and sell new types of arts-based products previously unrealised. I believe innovation researchers can help to identify these innovations. One way to do this is to look for a new combination of artistic conventions being used by a group of artists, provide a brief description of the new combination, archive video demonstrations and/or image examples, and organise the data into a publicly searchable and accessible database. Based on this theory, researchers should be able to identify new art forms by looking for evidence of social and institutional endorsement of a new form of art. That's exactly how I found *Hiplet*; a new combination of hip-hop dance and ballet practice created by art innovator Homer Bryant, first pioneered by a group of young black dancers in Chicago, diffused broadly on social media in 2016, socially endorsed by some hip-hop and ballet dancers, and now institutionally endorsed and supported by The Joyce Foundation, the Illinois Arts Council agency, and the National Endowment for the Arts.

The theory of art movement innovation should matter to innovation researchers because new art movements are social innovations that can help artists to build community. Art movements can increase artists' communal and associative relationships with one another. They can increase artists' access to shared social, economic, and cultural resources. They can also increase artists' ability to take collective action. Based on this theory, researchers should be able to identify new art movements by looking for evidence of the formation of collective artistic identities. Social media is a great place to start this research because there are so many collective artistic identities organised as private groups on platforms like Facebook and LinkedIn. That's how I found the *Weird Art Group* movement, created by art movement innovators Jaimi Fleming and Daniel Tyrrell, which on March 30, 2022, had 50.5k members in their Facebook group.

The theory of audience experience innovation should matter to innovation researchers because new audience experience designs can trigger new types of esthetic experience(s). These new experience innovations can rescue arts presenting from ritual. They can provide arts audiences with a new way to experience ancient works of art perceived to be old, uninteresting, and/or outdated. They can also help arts administrators develop new audiences for the arts. Based on this theory, researchers should be able to identify new audience experience designs if they look for shared changes in how specific groups of arts organisations are presenting works of art. That's how I recognised punchdrunk's *Sleep No More* as a new audience experience design that is changing how immersive theater is being presented around the world.

## Implications for entrepreneurship education

Theories of innovation in the arts should matter to entrepreneurship educators because innovation and entrepreneurship are complementary processes. When practiced together, they can result in increased production and distribution. They can also provoke widespread change(s) in specific industries. Given the mutually beneficial relationship between innovation and entrepreneurship practice, formal theories of innovation in the arts should be required reading and discussion for students in entrepreneurship courses, because they can help students to identify some innovations in the arts as entrepreneurship opportunities.

For example, the theory of art innovation can help students recognise new art forms as profit-making opportunities. Think about it. Consumers of art share a desire for arts-based products, and new art forms present entrepreneurs with opportunities to create and deliver new product options to customers and consumers. Students can exploit these profit-making opportunities by being amongst the first to create a market for arts-based products associated with a new art form, and by being amongst the first to deliver those products to customers and consumers in exchange for their money. Berry Gordy did this in the 1950s by recognising rhythm and blues (R&B) as a new style of music (i.e., the art innovation) popular amongst young black Americans. Gordy exploited this profit-making opportunity by being amongst the first to mass-produce the music of young black R&B artists (i.e., the arts-based products). Afterward, Gordy used crossover strategies to shape young white Americans' cultural tastes and preferences for his commercial brand of R&B music (i.e., market creation). Finally, Gordy sold this music (i.e., product delivery) primarily to young black and white R&B consumers in America throughout the 1960s. This is how Motown Records became one of the most successful black-owned businesses and one of the most influential independent record companies in American history.

For students interested in developing arts organisations, the theory of art movement innovation can help them to recognise an opportunity to help artists with shared artistic goals get organised. Recall that art movements are social innovations that start as informal organisations. Research in art history suggests that most art movements without formal organisational structures decline and dissolve fairly quickly. Formal arts organisations can provide members of an art movement with written membership roles and responsibilities, written policies and procedures for carrying out collective artistic action, written internal membership privileges and benefits, a mission statement that communicates purpose and vision, and a governance structure that can oversee activities of support staff. In addition, a motion towards legal incorporation can provide members of an art movement with access to new forms of financial capital, such as grant funding earmarked for not-for-profit organisations.

The theory of audience experience innovation can help students to recognise shared changes in arts presenting as an opportunity to stimulate economic activity in stagnant and/or declining economies of culture. Currently, in the United States, ticket sales to conventional opera performances are either stagnant or currently in decline. The same could be said for ticket sales to conventional ballet performances and conventional classical music performances. In many places around the world, the racial, age, and gender demographics of the population are changing. Today many members of younger generations perceive works of art once considered by opinion leaders in art worlds as masterpieces to be uninteresting, outdated, and irrelevant. Students need to recognise these global changes in perceptions of art as well as global changes in arts attendance. Students need to recognise that many of the conventional ways of arts presenting are no longer triggering a unique sensory experience for audiences. Students also need to recognise that many of the endorsed ways of arts presenting have never taken the accessibility needs of disabled audience members into account. For all these reasons, arts entrepreneurship educators in particular need to help students develop and test new ways of arts presenting. My theory of audience experience innovation can provide students with guidance and instruction.

## Call to action

Should anyone have an interest in pursuing any of these suggested research goals or educational initiatives, I provide consulting. Please send consulting inquiries to the email address dr.white@innovationinthearts.com. In addition, you can always learn about new art forms, new art movements and new audience experience designs emerging from around the world by subscribing to my e-newsletter. For those who wish to subscribe or learn more, please visit www.innovationinthearts.com.

# Index

Note: Page numbers followed by 'n' refer to notes.

For Product Safety Concerns and Information please contact our EU
representative GPSR@taylorandfrancis.com
Taylor & Francis Verlag GmbH, Kaufingerstraße 24, 80331 München, Germany